How to Win at the Game of College

How to Win at the Game of College

Practical Advice from a College Professor

Ryan R. Otter, Ph.D.

Milroy Press

How to Win at the Game of College © 2010
by Ryan R. Otter.

First edition published 2010

Published by Milroy Press, Murfreesboro TN, USA

Visit our website at www.thecollegegameproject.org

ISBN-13: 978-0-9829352-0-0

Manufactured and printed in the United States of America

Dedication

To Professor Mary Barnum.

Acknowledgments

First and foremost I need to thank my wife Liz for her unconditional support and honest feedback throughout this entire project. Without you this book and The College Game Project wouldn't exist.

A special thanks to Eric VanGenderen for enjoying these projects as much as I do, it wouldn't be the same without you.

I want to thank Pam Otter, Mary Barnum, Alex Keefe, Bob Milroy, Kim Sadler, Cindy Lee, Lyn Powers, Spencer Powers, Becky Elrod, Amy Smith, Karen Adams, Nathan Dary, Chase Kohne, Gina Logue, George Murphy, Gay Burden, Rhonda Waller, Carla Hatfield, Heather Arrington, and Wes Houp for reviewing and editing this project. Your feedback and encouragement were essential in completing this book.

I would also like to thank the professional mentors I've had throughout my career. You've helped me in more ways than you probably know. Thank you Steve Klaine, Jim Oris, Cindy Lee, and Tom Burton.

Finally, I would like to thank my parents. You have supported even the craziest of my ideas and endeavors. Thank you for your encouragement. I love you both.

Contents

Introduction

What does it mean to succeed at college? Most people would say graduating in four years. Some would say graduation, no matter how long it takes. It's my hope that by the end of this book you will agree with me that graduation should <u>not</u> be your definition of success at college. **Success at college should not be defined by any single event, such as graduation, but rather by how well prepared you are for your chosen career**. This is why I define success at college as having a career goal and a strategic plan to achieve that goal by the time you graduate.

Think about the best strategy for tackling any big challenge and the answer is always the same. First, you break the problem down into small, manageable pieces. Then, figure out good solutions for each piece. And finally you decide the best way to put the pieces back together. In this book I will tackle the problem of college success using this strategy. I will break down the complicated problem of how to succeed in college into easy-to-understand pieces, address each piece individually and in the end discuss how to best put the pieces back together. When I am finished, you will see that with the right mindset and right techniques you can succeed at college and set yourself up for long-term career success.

I'm a sports guy, so it is easy for me to relate things to sports, and because of this I tend to view everything as a game. In this book I am going to relate the game of college to the game of basketball. Imagine you don't know how to play the game of basketball. How would you tackle the complicated challenge of learning how to play basketball if you didn't know anything about it? If you really think about it, there are three major components you need to know in order to learn any game. First, you need to know the major tools and rules of the game (i.e. ball, basket, foul...etc). Second, you need to know who the other key people are in the game (i.e., teammates, opponents, coaches, referees, fans....etc). Third, you need to have a strategy on how you plan to win the game. These are the three major components you need to know in order to learn and win any game you don't know how to play.

This book is designed to teach you a new game that you likely don't know much about, the game of college. What do you currently know about college? Where have you gotten your advice on how you should approach college? Who are the other major people in your game? Should you communicate with each of these people the same way? Should you plan out all four years before you even start? Should you wait until you figure out exactly what you want to do professionally before you pick a major? Who should you live with in the dorms? How much partying is too much partying? If these questions aren't already running through your head, perhaps they should be. These are all very common questions for those about to enter college, and for a lot of students already in college. Each of these questions is important and needs to be addressed if you're planning on succeeding at college. In this book I will address most of these issues and purposely not address others.

I want to be very clear from the beginning exactly what this book is designed to help you with and what it's not going to address. **This book is designed to address the major components of college: the tools and rules of the college game, the other people that will be key to your success in college, and a strategy on how to achieve success in college.** This is not a book of shortcuts or easy ways to succeed. It's also not a book that's going to address how to get into college, how to pay for college, who you should live with, or how much you should party. It's not that I lack an opinion on these matters, or that I think they are unimportant. It's because each of these topics have no shortage of people willing to give advice and because none of these topics should be the focal point of your college years. What I have noticed, after spending nearly 10 years as a college student and subsequently entering the academic world as a college professor and researcher, is that I've never seen a good, universal, real-world guide on how to approach college that makes sense for everyone. Also, as a professor I continually see very good students struggle with the same issues year after year that I believe can be easily fixed by simply understanding some of the basic rules, knowing the key players, and having a good strategy. The goal of this book is to address common student issues and lay out a good, universal real-world approach to college that can help all students, regardless of career path.

All the advice I give in this book is based on my personal experience in life, nothing more. I believe that spending the last 13 years of my life in college, in one capacity or another, has given me multiple perspectives on college, and it's my hope that my experiences and advice can make your college experience as fulfilling as possible.

In my experience, the best way to explain and break down the complicated new game of college is to describe first the strategy for success, then lay out the major tools and rules of the game, followed by a breakdown of the other key players in the game. Lastly, after we've broken everything down and explained the details of each piece, we will step back and look at how to put the pieces together. In the end, I hope this book gives you a new perspective on college with a clear focus on what a successful college experience means, and the confidence to succeed at this important game.

Section 1
The Strategy for Success

Introduction

What's the difference between a good basketball team and a great basketball team (assuming they have the same level of talent)? The difference is that a great team will have both a good strategy *and* the ability to execute. In the game of basketball this is easy to see. Ever wonder why the best basketball teams continually win year after year? This is no accident. The game of basketball is a team sport, and in order to be great, the team needs to play well together. Coaches instill a mindset in their players that leads to every player knowing how they fit into the team so they can play at the highest level possible. The coach comes up with a strategy for the team, and the players must execute that strategy in order for the team to win. Without a winning strategy the team will lose. Without good execution of that winning strategy the team will lose. Both good strategic planning and execution are necessary to win.

The game of college is no different than the game of basketball, in the sense that you need both a winning strategy and good execution in order to win. The strategy I explain in this book will focus on both of these vital pieces. The first key point, setting a career goal, focuses entirely on explaining a strategic plan for winning at the game of college. Key points 2 and 3 focus how to best execute that plan. Sounds simple? It's not. It takes hard work and the willingness to ask some difficult questions about yourself and what you actually think about your future. Here's the good news - by utilizing this strategy you will be on the path for long-term success no matter what major or career you choose. In order to understand how to use this strategy we need to look at each key point individually and break it down so it makes sense in the real world.

Chapter 1
Set a Career Goal

If you graduate college and start work when you're 25 and plan on working until you're 60, you will be part of the workforce for 35 years. If you were to work an average of 50 weeks a year, 40 hours a week for those 35 years, you would have worked 70,000 hours or eight straight years with no breaks. That's 35 years of your life, twice as long as a high school senior has been alive. In fact, if you break that down even further, over that same 35-year span, aside from sleeping you will spend more time at work than any place else. Add up the numbers; they don't lie. I truly ask you to think about this and let it soak in a bit, because when people do, one of two things typically happens. Either they look at the numbers and get horribly depressed thinking about all the time they will have to spend at a job to support their lifestyle and family, or they look at it as an opportunity to accomplish great things. Just imagine for a second what you could accomplish if you were given 35 years to work on something that you loved and had a passion for. This difference leads me to ask you a question: is there a difference between a job and a career?

The answer is absolutely, there is a difference between a job and a career! If you pick up a dictionary and read their definitions it may be hard to tell the difference, but ask any person in the workforce, and I'll bet they will agree there is a difference. **The difference between a job and a career has little to do with *what* profession you choose, and a lot to do with the *attitude* you take toward your profession**. Typically, a job is something that's done with the main focus being the money you make. The actual work being done doesn't really matter that much, it's simply a means to make money. If given an opportunity to make better money with the same hours, switching jobs would be easy, since there is little vested interest in the work being done. In contrast to a job, with a career you have a vested interest in the work being done, you have a goal of long-term progress within the field, you have passion for your work, and you make money while doing it.

I advise that when you're thinking about which major to pick you continually think about what career you want rather than what job you might get. I know this may sound like a trivial switching of words, but I assure you it's not. By choosing to use certain words on a regular basis that you clearly understand, you can begin to change the way you think. Too often people use words without really knowing the meaning of those words. The idea of using different words in place of others is a common theme throughout this book and is a technique that can help you if you're trying to change your attitude about anything.

Getting the career you want starts with having a career goal. In my experience, most people in college don't have a career goal, and those that do tend to set their goals too low. I'm going to use a story about one of my former students, Mike, to highlight this problem.

I ran into Mike, now a junior, on campus about a year after he had taken my Introduction to Biology course. Mike was a good student, and I had the pleasure of getting to know him during the semester he was in my class. As Mike and I were catching up, he was excited to tell me that he had taken my advice and set out a plan for his future and that he now had a career goal. He told me that he had decided he wanted to be an economics teacher in high school. I of course was excited for him and congratulated him on planning his future and then asked him "What's your career goal?"

Mike looked at me confused, thinking he just told me what his goal was and answered, "to be a economics teacher in high school".

I then asked him "In your entire life as a student, have you ever had a bad teacher?"

He laughed and said "Yeah, more than I can count."

Then I asked, "Have you ever had a really great teacher?"

Mike answered, "A few".

I replied with another question, "How hard is it to become a teacher?"

He knew right away what I was getting at and answered "not very hard".

Thousands of students graduate and become teachers every year, but how many become <u>excellent</u> teachers? I told Mike that with his drive, motivation, and talent just becoming a teacher is way too low of a goal. I told him to think of all the teachers he has ever had that weren't very good and asked him if that was the kind of teacher he wanted to be. The advice I gave Mike was simple. I told him his career goal should not be to be an economics teacher; that's too low of a goal; I told him his career goal should be to be a kick-ass economics teacher. A teacher who influences people, a teacher who inspires others....just like the person he was thinking about when I asked if he ever had a really great teacher in his life. Now that's a career goal.

Just being a teacher in my opinion is too low of a goal. In fact, graduating with any degree is too low of a goal, and that includes undergraduate degrees, masters degrees, Ph.Ds, M.Ds., D.V.Ms....it doesn't matter. **Graduation should not be the long-term career goal for anyone.** Career goals need to be goals that go beyond college. This way your drive, focus, and passion won't decrease after graduation. Graduation is merely a stepping-stone.

I'm going to tell you something that you've probably never heard and that you may not want to hear, but it's the truth.....graduating from college isn't all that hard for even an average student. By putting a modest amount of effort into your studies, you likely will pass most of your classes (I didn't say you'll get A's) and make your way to graduation. Of course, as you pick a major and get into upper division courses they get harder, but they are still manageable. **If passing your classes and getting to graduation is the highest goal you've set for yourself, I think you are setting your standards too low.**

Think about the conversation I had with Mike. Have you ever had a bad teacher? I'm going to guess that the answer is yes, and that you've probably had more than one. You can think about that conversation and substitute any profession for teaching and the answer will be the same. For example, take accounting. There are good accountants and bad accountants. Just graduating and becoming an accountant is too low of a goal. Take a moment to think about your experience with other professionals such as doctors, coaches, and counselors. Do you think the really good ones just happened by chance? I have very high expectations for Mike; in fact, I have very high expectations for all my students. **You should have high expectations for yourself, because without high expectations, you can never become great.**

The problem with setting graduation as your highest goal is wasted opportunity. During your college years you will have an unbelievable amount of time to experience new things. To completely ignore or wait until your senior year to think about life after graduation is setting yourself up for long-term disappointment. The time and energy you spend early on thinking about life after graduation can pay big dividends in the future. Later in the section, I will introduce what I call the 50:50 concept, which will teach you how to spend your energy and time on both classroom and "real-world" learning so you don't waste opportunity.

I have one more major point I need to address before I introduce the exercises that can help you pick the right career goal, and that is the definition of the phrase "hard work". I hear this phrase frequently from many students, and it has made me think carefully about what it means. Of course, we are all told that if we work hard and stay focused, good things will happen. Although I agree, I think at the college level this phrase needs to be re-defined. When I ask students what it means to work hard in college, the most common answer is "to study hard and get good grades", which makes sense....if your career goal is to graduate. Then I ask them what they plan to do after they graduate and the answer is typically the same.... "get a job". This is the perfect example of setting goals too low and not having a strategy for life after college, even if you worked hard to graduate. By setting a long-term career goal, and having a strategy to accomplish that goal, the definition of working hard changes compared to when the goal is simply to graduate. I'm going to use an example to demonstrate how the definition of hard work changes when you have a career goal and a strategy. My example will focus on two people, Andy and Matt, who are both lost in the woods.

Andy and Matt are lost deep in the woods, miles and miles away from anyone else. Both Andy and Matt have the exact same goal....get un-lost as fast as possible. Matt decides to run as fast as he can and when he comes to a fork in the path, he makes the decision on which path to take very quickly and continues on. He is working hard, very hard. Running as fast as he can, with no idea where he is going, he is working really hard on getting there (except he doesn't know where *there* is). Andy, on the other hand, decides to make a strategic plan. He decides to make a map of what he knows and devise a strategy to get un-lost. His strategy is to hike to the top of the nearest hilltop and see if there is a village in sight. He realizes that just thinking about hiking isn't going to get him to the top of the hill; he now must execute his strategy. When Andy gets to the top of the first hilltop he finds out there was not a village in sight, but he notices a river in the valley below him. He takes what he has learned and modifies his strategy. His new plan is to run to the valley to see if there are any boats by the river. At the same time Andy has been working on planning and executing his strategy, Matt has been running as fast as he can. Matt's plan is relying on the hope and luck that by running as fast as possible he will run into someone that can help him.

In this scenario, who gets "un-lost" first: Andy or Matt? If I'm a betting man, my money is on Andy. Is it possible that Matt gets un-lost first? Yes, but is it more likely to happen? Probably not. Both are working hard, but not in the same way.

The scenario with Andy and Matt may sound silly, but it highlights the idea that working hard does not equal working smart. Most college students are completely lost on what career to pursue or what they could even see themselves doing for the next 30 years....they are lost in the woods (except that the woods in this example is in their own mind). Most college students take the strategy taken by Matt, which is to run as fast as possible through the woods and hope something gets them un-lost. They are banking on the idea that hard work alone is all they need and the rest will take care of itself. In the college game Matt's strategy equates to the attitude of: if I study really hard, even with no understanding of where it's going to take me or really where I might end up, then everything will just work out. Put another way, as long as I get good grades, everything will just work out. I find this strategy and use of the phrase "hard work" to be rather troubling because with it you are waiting for something to happen to you. I strongly disagree with this attitude and teach those that I work with that hard work is important, but it's just as valuable to know what you are working to achieve. Getting good grades is only one piece of a much bigger puzzle. Taking time to figure out what

16

you actually like, setting a high career goal, and devising a strategic plan to achieve your goals are just as valuable as getting good grades. No matter how much hard work you do it's extremely difficult to become successful if you don't have a plan on how to get there. Of course, there are exceptions in which students stumble onto a career they love, but it's rare. I suggest not leaving something so important to luck or chance.

A movie quote constantly goes through my mind when I first sit down with a student who has never thought about their career goals before. The quote comes from the great comedy movie *Office Space*: "[People] work just hard enough not to get fired". I find this to be quite accurate when dealing with students who work hard, but have no idea what they are working towards. It makes perfect sense if you take a minute and think about it. How long can you stay interested in something if you have no idea why you're doing it? This is exactly what is going on when you are working hard in college without a career goal. Without a career goal in mind, working hard becomes boring and annoying because you have no idea where it's going to take you. One solution to this is to stop working hard until you get a goal, and unfortunately this is the path taken by most students. Students wait for something to "hit them" and inspire them. They wait for classes to show them what major they should choose, which usually results in students picking a major for the wrong reasons. The other solution is to actively seek the right career goal and aggressively decide if it's what you want to do. This is the direction I recommend; combining hard work with a high career goal in mind.

What's the Right Career Goal for You?

Picking the right career goal is a complicated task. Just like any complicated task, we are going to address it by breaking it down into smaller pieces, work on understanding each of the pieces and then put all the pieces back together in the end. To best address this task, we need to separate it into two phases. Phase 1: choosing a goal and Phase 2: determining if you made the right choice in Phase 1.

Unfortunately, there is no test you can take that will tell you what the right career goal for you should be. It's going to take hard work, it's going to be frustrating at times, and it's going to make you think in ways you've probably never thought before. Mainly, you will have to think a lot about how you view yourself. There is one vital point to picking the right career goal that you need to keep in mind at all times: **your career goal MUST be chosen by you and no one else**. I'm not saying to avoid getting advice from other people (as you'll see throughout the book, it's quite the opposite of that), but, in the end, the final decision is yours and no one else's....not your parent's, not your professor's, not your friend's....its yours and yours alone. Right now, I'm guessing you don't feel like you know enough or have enough information to make such a huge decision like setting your career goal, which is probably true. This is where the two phases for picking the right career goal come in. So let's start breaking down the problem of not knowing which career is right for you so you can start putting an answer together.

Phase 1:
How to Choose a Career Goal

Since you are the one making the decision about which career goal you want to set, it's essential you're honest with yourself. I know there is a lot of pressure put on you to say the right things in front of the right people, to act a certain way, to dress a certain way, etc. I also know that a lot of the time what you do in certain situations isn't exactly what you think is right or what you think you should be doing. This is natural and all part of growing up and being a kid. What I am describing in this book is not written for kids. If you're not willing to ask yourself the hard questions about what you actually think, be honest with your answers, and act the way you think is right, there is no need to continue reading this section or this book.

I commonly ask students how they view themselves, and what I've learned from this simple question has been both extremely enlightening and scary. The most common answer I hear is that they don't understand the question, which after digging a little deeper is another way of saying they've never thought about it. So what I do next is ask this question: "Do you view yourself as a man (or woman) or a kid?"

Over the past three years I would say that over 95% of students always answer the same way...as a kid. This common answer has scared me because it made me question how I could ever expect students to be honest with themselves, make life-changing decisions about their future, or focus on their career if they view themselves as kids? The answer is I couldn't. This made me realize that **in order for any person to properly execute any strategy they must have the right mindset, and without the right mindset even the best strategic plans will fail.**

I don't know a polite way to put this, so I'm not going to try: **you are not a kid**. If you are starting college you need to understand that **you are not a kid anymore**. **It doesn't matter whether you still want to be a kid or not, you are not a kid**. I'm not going to lean on the argument that by law you are a grown adult, legally responsible for your actions, although that is absolutely true. I'm simply going to tell you that in order to make good decisions for yourself, about your career, and your life, you must view yourself as a grown man or woman who is willing to be honest with yourself and not view yourself as a kid. This isn't an easy task, but a necessary task if you want to pick the right career goal for yourself. This way of thinking is not something that happens overnight. A huge part of Phase 1 is understanding how not to think like a kid any more, and it all centers around being truthful and honest with yourself.

In order to pick the right career goal you need to concentrate on honestly answering two questions. What do I like? And why do I like it? By honestly answering each of these questions, you can start to determine which career path is right for you, or more commonly, you can start to figure out which career paths are not right for you. Either way, you can end up with a well thought out goal and a strategy to achieve that goal.

Although it may sound easy to answer questions honestly about what you really like and why you like it, you need to realize this may not be a simple task. Most students just leaving high school struggle with their identity. In my experience, there is an easy trick that helps students be honest with themselves and figure out who they really are, which makes choosing a career goal much easier. The trick is privacy. For most people to be completely 100% honest with themselves they need to know their thoughts and ideas won't be seen by anyone else.

Privacy is the key to honesty. In the Facebook and text message world that you live in, where people like to share every detail of what happens to them, privacy may seem like a thing of the past, but it doesn't have to be. Although keeping things private may not be what everyone else is doing, neither is setting a career goal or thinking about their future. **If you can only be 100% honest with yourself by keeping your thoughts private, then keep your thoughts private. Without complete honesty you can't expect to make the right choices when it comes to your career goal.**

Even if you are 100% honest with yourself do you have enough experience to pick what you want to do professionally with the rest of your life? I'm going to assume the advice you've gotten so far about picking a major or picking the right career sounds something like this: "pick something you love and you can see yourself doing the rest of your life". Sounds like good advice, but do you have enough experience to make such a huge decision? Did high school really show you how the professional world works? I'm guessing not. One of the main reasons I've written this book is because the advice most students receive about setting career goals doesn't include any strategy on how to pick the right one, except for guessing. This is too big a decision to guess on; you are going to spend more hours living with this decision than any other in your lifetime (except for sleeping). This is why I've developed the career goal exercise to help you gain the experience and information necessary to make a good, informed decision about picking the right career goal. In this exercise, all you need to do is focus on being honest and follow your gut feel.

The Career Goal Exercise

Over the last decade nearly all colleges have adopted a website design that can give you a huge advantage in picking a career goal, if you know how to use it properly. Nearly all colleges build their websites the same way; they have a welcome page and basically the same links to categories such as academics, admissions, current students, future students, research...etc. Most colleges are involved in research, and this is where you can really benefit from your college's website, even when you're not on campus. Though some college websites will have a direct link to their research page, I suggest not using it. I think there is a better way to start narrowing down areas that you may want to pursue as a career.

The goal of this exercise is to gain the information and experience necessary to make an informed decision about what career goal is best for you. I highly recommend this exercise be done in private and not shared with anyone until the entire exercise is completed.

Step 1 – Find a list of links to all departments on campus. On every college homepage there will be a link for "academics". Click this link. This will send you to a page that will either list all the departments on campus or it will send you to a page with another link to get you there. If you have problems finding this webpage, look up the main phone number for the college under the "contacts" link on the homepage, call and ask someone how to locate the webpage that lists all the departments on campus.

Step 2 - Start at the top and work your way down…using your gut feel. Take a single piece of paper and by simply looking at the name of the department, use your gut feel and ask yourself this question "does this sound interesting to me?" You don't have to think about why it does or doesn't sound interesting, just think whether it does or not. If the answer is even a little bit yes, write the department name down on the paper; if your immediate answer is no, don't write it down and go on to the next department on the list. That's it. One big key to this exercise, although it may seem trivial, is to write in your own handwriting. Don't type your answers. Do it in your own handwriting on plain white paper.

Step 3 – Learn from faculty research interests. Take your paper and for every department you have listed start a new piece of paper with the name of each department on top. For example, if on your paper you wrote down 15 departments, you will need 15 new pieces of paper, each with a different department name on top. Start with the first department you wrote down, take your new piece of paper with that department written on top and click the link into that department's webpage. Next, you want to find a list of the faculty working in that department, which is typically found by clicking on either the "faculty" link or the "faculty & staff" link. Once you have a list of faculty in that department, you need to find a faculty member's individual research interests. This may already be displayed once you click on the 'faculty' link, but likely you will need to click on each individual faculty name. Now, do the same thing you did in step 2, go name by name, reading each persons research interests. If their research description is interesting to you, write down that person's name, a one-sentence summary of their research, and their email address, and move on to the next person. Again, use your gut feel. Don't try and reason out why it's interesting, or whether or not you can make money doing it. Just follow your gut, if it's interesting write it down. If it's not, don't write it down. Do this for every department you wrote down.

Note: On some websites you may need to click on a research link to access the proper pages for a list of research faculty. Again, if you have trouble finding the right web pages at your college, look up the main phone number for the college, under the "contacts" link on the homepage, call and ask someone how to locate the web pages you need.

Step 4 – Rank your lists. Once you've completed searching all the research interests take some time and look at your lists. For some people this may be 20 pieces of paper full of names and interests. For others this may be two or three pieces of paper. The number of names you write down is irrelevant; being honest with yourself, however, is everything in this exercise. Once you have these lists, take time to rank the professors you find most interesting in order from most interesting to the least interesting based on their research. *This should not to be a difficult exercise.* This is <u>not</u> designed as a decision making list, but rather a way to find out what you actually find interesting. *This step can be completed on a computer if you see fit, but make sure steps 2 and 3 are done by hand.*

Step 5 – Contact faculty members that you find interesting. Have you ever met someone who didn't like to talk about themselves? Likely the answer is no. Most people do, and faculty members at your college are no exception. Professors have made the decision to make their career goals focused on teaching and research. You can utilize their experience and take advantage of their expertise to help you make a good decision about your career goals.

You now have in your possession a list of your interests that you need more information on before you can even consider making a well-informed decision about a career goal. You have the contact information of someone who has more experience than you and has chosen a career path based on helping students just like you. This is the perfect formula for you to gain the information you need to help you make a good career decision.

There is no website in the world that can give you more information than a good conversation. That's why step 5 is focused on setting up face-to face meetings with those faculty members you share an interest with. Using the email addresses you have from your list in step 4, you need to write very concise, clear, and professional emails to the professors you would like to meet. For example, if I had an interest in Dr. Roberts' research, an engineering professor whose research interest is the making of long-term batteries for storage of solar energy, I would write an email similar to this:

Dr. Roberts

My name is Ryan Otter, I am a freshman here at Meekster College. I've been working on narrowing down the right career path to pursue. I have an interest in alternative energy and am excited to gain some insight and possibly some experience in this field to know if it's a good fit for me. Would you be willing to have a short meeting with me to discuss some of your research and possible careers I may pursue in this area? Also, is there anyone else at the College you would recommend I talk with?

Ryan Otter
Email address: otter@meekster.edu

Let's take a look at the email I wrote and point out some of the keys to writing a good introduction email. First and foremost, the email must be written in a professional manner and in a professional style. Do not use text-message words or shorthand of any kind. Since you are in complete control of when you send an email, it's not a bad idea to have someone else read an email like this before sending it if you have any doubt about its professionalism. Note that I start off by introducing myself. I give a bit of information about myself and why I'm writing the email. This is key, because professors work with a lot of students, and this will let them know from the very beginning who you are and what you are looking for.

Next, the email is direct and to the point. This shows very clearly that you are taking this seriously, that you've put real thought into the decision to write this email and that you are willing to ask for help. Next, look at the last sentence of the email because this is an essential component. The professors you are emailing likely know the best people on campus in their given field. This is a very quick and easy way to understand the network that exists on campus in any research area. Last, and I can't stress this point enough, **there is no substitute for enthusiasm**. People in general, and especially professors, will go to extraordinary lengths to help students who show enthusiasm. I can tell you personally that when I have students come into my office that is interested in making themselves better, I will bend over backwards to help that person any way I can. When people show me they are willing to ask for help and do what's necessary to get what they want, I will do everything I can to help them succeed.

I would be misguiding you if I didn't point out that you will likely not get a 100% return on your emails. Some professors are just busy, some are lazy with email, and some just simply won't send you something back. This should not discourage you. If you are focused on setting a career goal you should not see this as a dead end, but a mere bump in the road. This is a great example of how the real world operates after you are done with college; you are not always going to get the response you want or even a response at all. You must realize that this cannot slow you down, and that it's just part of the game you are playing. You can't take a professors' lack of response as a personal insult or a personal failure on your part. As I will point out later in this book, personal and professional relationships are different and the rules for each are different. Communication with professors in this manner is 100% professional, so be sure not to take it personally.

Once a meeting has been set up you will want to maximize this opportunity. Like all professional meetings you need to be well prepared. For a meeting like this you should be ready for three things. 1) Be prepared to ask questions. 2) Be prepared to answer questions. 3) Be genuine and honest at all times. Different professors have different personalities, and unless you have prior knowledge of a professor's personality, it's best to be prepared on all fronts. I would suggest preparing a list of two or three questions you can ask the professor you are meeting about their research. Take time to learn some basic knowledge about the professor's field of study prior to meeting them. You don't have to become an expert, but know enough to have an intelligent conversation. Do not ask super vague questions like, "why do you like science?" or "is it fun working in this field?" Remember, you asked to have this meeting. Take yourself seriously and take full advantage of the time the professor is spending with you. I also suggest being prepared to answer some common questions that may be asked of you, like why does this field interest you? What experience do you have? Do you have a career goal in mind? At all times be honest. Don't just tell the professor what you think they want to hear. At this point you have committed to nothing and have nothing to lose and everything to gain, so be honest and gain as much useful information as you possibly can.

Be aware that step 5 may take months to complete if you have a wide variety of interests. The time frame of completing these steps is completely dependent on you, but once you've completed them, you should have enough good information to make an informed decision about your career goal.

Choosing Your Career Goal

If you have completed the career goal exercise you are ready to set your career goal. You now possess a list of your interests and information directly from experts in the fields you're interested in. You will never know everything, and you will always want to know more before making a decision like choosing a career goal. You need to recognize this is human nature and that you are better off picking a career goal and moving forward to the next phase than not making a decision. Remember, the next phase is determining if you made the right choice.

The best advice I can give you is that **your choice of career goals should be made using your gut feel**. You know yourself better than anyone else. You just have to believe that what you feel is right. **Write down your career goal in your own handwriting on a piece of paper and keep it in a private place**. Don't set your goal low and don't make graduation or any other event your goal. Remember, you're going to be the only one who reads this goal, so be honest and write down the truth about what you want to attain. Your career goal is yours; it doesn't have to make sense to anyone else but you.

Before we move on to Phase 2, I want to finish with a story about a very common problem that holds a lot of students back from setting their career goal. Justin was a sophomore in one of the first classes I ever taught as a professor. He stopped by my office to ask me questions about what biologists do once they graduate from college because he was looking into different majors. Of course I was excited because a student was showing interest in what I was doing. I gave him a good overview of the different careers biologists can have and told him very honestly that it really just depended on what he was interested in. Then I asked him a very direct question: "How do you plan on picking a major and how do you plan on deciding what you're going to do after graduation?"

Justin's answer was "I don't know, I figure that's what college is supposed to show me. I'll take a bunch of classes and it will just hit me."

It was the "it will just hit me" part that really stood out in my mind. That was pretty much the end of our conversation, and I can't remember ever having another meeting with Justin, but I thought about his answer for a long time and it made me realize three very interesting things about *how* college works. The first two we will discuss right now, and the third I will cover later in this section.

The first interesting thing that my conversation with Justin made me realize was that things rarely, if ever, just hit a person. You never hear of someone accomplishing something great by just waiting for something to happen. The one thing all people who accomplish great things have in common is that they worked hard toward something specific. Interestingly enough, in a lot of those cases, their original goal was not where they ended up. This made me realize very clearly that **the journey is more important than the destination.** I've heard this saying before, but to be honest, I never understood what it meant. Now I see the value in this simple statement. It's nearly impossible to accomplish anything great without having a destination picked out (your career goal), but it's the attitude and the steps you take toward achieving that goal (the journey) that are the most important. You can't wait for something to pop magically into your mind and

33

show you what you want to do with the rest of your life. If you do, you're going to continually feel lost. When you wait for something great to happen to you, you will continually be disappointed when nothing great happens. The truth is that you are always going to feel lost unless you decide to set a destination (a career goal) and have a journey mapped out on how to get there (a strategy).

The second interesting thing I realized after my conversation with Justin was that no college course has ever taught me what life was going to be like in the real world (remember, I spent almost 10 straight years taking college courses). Now, this may not be true for all majors, but I'm going to be conservative and say that 98% of college courses don't train you for what the real working world is going to be like. The truth is college courses are not designed to teach you how the real world works. **College courses are designed to teach the fundamentals that are essential to understanding concepts, not show you what a career is going to be like in the real world.** If you think that college courses alone are going to give you the preparation and experience you need to succeed in your chosen profession, you are just plain wrong.

I know this may sound like I'm giving you advice opposite of what I gave you earlier when describing how valuable professors can be in giving you information to help you set you career goals, but it's not. Make sure you understand the difference between a professor and a college course. As a professor, I can tell you that my goals for every class I teach are very clear and <u>never</u> have they been to teach my students how the real world works. It's simply not the goal of the course. So why would you only use classroom information to pick a major or more importantly, a career goal? It doesn't make sense. So what information should you use and where do you get it from? You need to trust yourself and the people (not the courses) within your areas of interest to help you pick the right career goal.

Examples of Good Career Goals

- To be a kick ass teacher. One who influences students in a positive way and prepares them for the future.
- To be a kick ass heart surgeon. One who understands everything there is to know about the human heart and how it works.
- To be a kick ass Information Technology (IT) consultant. One who always makes the lives of people they work for better.
- To be a kick ass accountant. One who helps a business grow and run the way it should.

Phase 2:
How to Know You've Chosen the
Right Career Goal

Finishing Phase 1 and writing down your career goal (especially for the first time) may be the most difficult part of the entire strategy, so be sure to take a deep breath and congratulate yourself. But be careful not to celebrate too long. Now you need to figure out if the decision you made about your career goal was the right one. Like everything else so far this may sound like a near impossible task, and just like everything else we are going to tackle this challenge the same way....break it down into pieces that you can solve and put them back together.

A major fear of most people that are genuinely interested is setting high career goals centers around the question of "what if I picked the wrong goal?" I developed the 50:50 concept to directly address this question so you can know you made the right decision. This decision is too important to leave to luck or chance. You want to *know*, not guess, that you made the right choice.

The 50:50 Concept

The 50:50 concept focuses on three words: **energy**, **experience** and **information**. **Experience** and **information** are the keys to gaining the self-confidence and knowledge that you've made the right decision about your career goal. It takes a smart use of your **energy** to gather the right **information** and **experience**.

Everyday you have a limited amount of energy, and you choose to give a certain amount of that energy to dozens of different things....family, friends, working out, school, video games...etc. Understanding that you have, in any given day, a limited amount of energy and that you <u>choose</u> how you spend it is vital. You can think of it as a game of percentages. Everyday you start with 100% of your energy for that day and even though some days you will have more than others, each day you only have 100%. Notice that I didn't use the word time, I used the word energy, and there is a very clear difference between these two words. Just because you are spending time on something doesn't mean you're spending energy on it. For example, you can spend 3 hours staring at a book and not put any energy into learning what's written. You need to make a conscious choice on how much energy you want to spend on college, and as I'll explain in this section the energy you should put towards college is more than just going to class.

37

I'm not going to tell you how much of your daily energy should go into college. Everybody is different and everybody's college situation is different. Some students have to work through college, while some don't, some play sports, some love video games, some love to party, etc. **How much energy you decide to put towards college is completely your choice**, but it's a choice that you should at least recognize you are making. The amount of time you spend on college never "just happens"; it's your choice.

The 50:50 concept focuses on how to best use the energy you choose to put towards college by maximizing your opportunities. **The 50:50 concept is based on the premise that 50 percent of all energy put into college should be spent on "academics" and 50 percent of all energy put into college should be spent on "career".** I define "academics" as all activities focused around the classroom and "career" as all non-academic activities focused on your career goal. By utilizing this concept you will have both the information and real world experience about your career goal to know if you've picked the right one.

The energy you spend on "academics" and "career" deserves an equal share of your attention during your time spent at college. Let's start with "academics" since it's the category you're most familiar with. I consider all activities focused around the classroom to fit into the "academic" category, no matter what subject you are studying. Activities such as going to class, studying, class projects, homework, quizzes, exams, and laboratories are all included in this category. The "academic" category is essential for long-term success for multiple reasons. First, the classroom information you are taught will give you the fundamentals of a given topic, and there is no way you can be great at anything without knowing the fundamentals. Second, without "academics" you won't be able to graduate from college, which is probably an essential step to achieving your career goal. Let's be honest, in today's world just knowing information is only going to get you so far. **In the modern world you need to demonstrate that you not only know the right information (based on the grades you get), but also that you can finish what you started (graduation).** I don't think I need to elaborate anymore than I have about the importance of "academics". If you're even reading this book you've probably been told the value of education repeatedly, so let's focus on the category that's just as important but not as well under-stood...."career".

When using the 50:50 concept, you should be spending 50% of all the energy you're putting into college towards your "career". As I mentioned earlier, I define the "career" category as all non-academic activities focused on your career goal. By focusing this much energy toward "career" you will gain the information and the necessary real-world experience to know if you have chosen the right career goal. **Another way to look at the "career" portion of the 50:50 concept is to view it as an aggressive attitude toward answering questions.** You need to actively and aggressively seek the answer to the question....did I pick the right career goal? To do this you need to rely on experts already working in the field you've chosen to give you the information necessary to understand what your career is *actually* going to be like in the real world. Examples of "career" activities include volunteering, interning, shadowing, interviewing, and working in the field.

      The biggest concern about any decision you make needs to be the quality of information you rely on. The "academic" and "career" categories of the 50:50 concept are no exception. In the "academic" portion you are relying on professors to give you accurate information. Professors are deemed good sources of information based on their track record. Professors have demonstrated they are experts in their field and have earned their credibility. In the "career" portion you need to rely on experts working in the field you have chosen to give you information about your career goal. You cannot rely on TV or people that have no experience in your chosen field to give you good information (that likely includes your parents). By following steps similar to those we laid out in the career goal exercise, you can easily find the best experts working in your chosen profession (see examples).

There are plenty of sources of information in this world, but not all of these sources are credible. You need to understand *where* the best pieces of information come from and aggressively go get the answers to your questions from those sources. It's also very helpful to recognize where bad information is coming from so you don't waste energy on it. This is an important point because most people are very willing to give you advice, but not all advice comes from a good source.

As I mentioned earlier you could view the "career" category of the 50:50 concept as an aggressive attitude toward answering the question "did you pick the right career goal?". To best answer this question you need to break that question into smaller, more direct questions and figure out the answer to each of the smaller questions. Once you have the answers to the smaller questions you can piece those answers together and decide if you picked the right career goal. **For all professions there are six questions (core questions) that you need to be able to answer before ever deciding if you've picked the right career goal.**

These core questions are generic questions that need to be tailored to your specific profession, as you will see in the examples.

Question #1) What specialty do I want to pursue?
Question #2) What is the day-to-day life like?
Question #3) What are the major perks of the career?
Question #4) What are the major downsides of the career?
Question #5) What salary range can I expect to make?
Question #6) Is the cost of training worth it in the end?

To show how the 50:50 concept works in the real world, we are going to look at multiple examples to highlight the flexibility of this concept and a common pitfall some students fall into. We will start with the example of two students, Jessica and Ashley. Jessica and Ashley are both freshman at the same college and have both always wanted to be doctors. People had always told each of them they were smart and that they would make great doctors. They both declared Pre-Med as their majors and were starting to work through their introductory courses with the hope that in four years they would apply to medical school and be well on their way to becoming doctors. Both had the same career goal: to become a great doctor. Jessica had chosen to use the 50:50 concept as described in this section and Ashley had chosen to take the classic approach to college, which focuses solely on classes and grades. Let's take a look at how each of them spent their energy and time at college and compare the information and experience gained by each student.

Jessica and Ashley both recognized that to get into medical school they needed really good grades and both were dedicated enough to commit whatever time it took to get those grades. So as far as energy spent on "academics" goes, they both were expending about the same. In fact, not only is the amount of energy spent on academics the same, likely the information gained by both was about the same. They likely took the same courses, likely with the same professors. Overall up to this point the two students look to be on the same road to the same place, and from Ashley's viewpoint (classic approach to college) she was doing everything she needed to do to help her obtain her career goal. However, from Jessica's viewpoint (50:50 concept) this is only half of what she needed to be doing with her college energy. Let's take a look at how Jessica spent the other half of her college energy.

The first thing Jessica probably realized when trying to figure out *how* to spend her "career" energy was that this was not a simple problem with a simple solution. She knew she didn't have enough good information or real-world experience to make a good, informed decision about being a doctor. The first thing Jessica needed to do is figure out if she actually wanted to be a doctor. Since she already had a career goal picked out, she was ready to start the 50:50 concept and decide if she made the right choice. Her first step was to tailor the six core questions specifically to her situation, for example:

-What medical specialty is the right one for me?
-What would my day-to-day life be like as a doctor?
-What are the major perks of being a doctor?
-What are the major downsides of being a doctor?
-What salary can I expect to make as a doctor?
-Is the cost of going through med school worth it in the end?

In Jessica's case, to properly apply the 50:50 concept, she needed to aggressively seek the answers to questions listed above. So let's take a look at her questions and figure out a good aggressive strategy for answering them. Don't forget, Jessica's goal in all this was to gain enough knowledge and real-world experience to know if she picked the right career goal of being a great doctor.

If Jessica were one of my students I would advise her to use the same strategy outlined in the career goal exercise, except modify it for questions she has. I would advise her to use an Internet search to list all the major medical specialties and use her gut feel to write down the specialties that were most interesting to her. I would then advise her to write down the name and phone number of *every* doctor whose office is within 50 miles (easily done with an

Internet search) and begin contacting each of the names on the list to ask if the doctor could find 15 minutes to spend with an interested student. Just like the situation with professors, some are not going to have time and some are. The doctors in the specialties she is interested in are the best sources of information for all of the questions she has. She must be prepared to ask the right questions and maximize the time experts give her to get the information she needs to make an informed decision. In order to make an informed decision on whether or not she picked the right career goal, **the general rule to follow is not to make a decision until you have the advice of <u>at least three different professionals</u> in the specialty you are interested in pursuing.** I know that seems like a lot, and something like that would take a lot of time, and you're right, it does. But there is no other way to get the information you need to make an informed decision about your career goal. **There is no short cut to making sure you've picked the right career goal**; it's going to take time and energy.

The other major advice I would give Jessica would be to **gain real world experience**. No classroom in the world can ever replace the information real world experience can give. College courses are not designed to teach you what happens in the real world, so you can't rely on them to give the answers to the questions you have. I would advise her to volunteer time to gain real world experience.

If an opportunity became available that could give her real world experience and a paycheck, that's great, but in the big picture, the experience is more valuable than the money. **Focus on gaining real world experience, even if it means taking no pay.** This is where having a clear career goal written down helps out. It can keep you focused on the long-term goal and serve as a reminder of *why* you are doing what you're doing. Remember, the goal is to get as much information and real world experience as possible to decide if you picked the right career goal. Keep that in mind and be willing to sacrifice time and energy to gain the best information and experience you can.

The examples of Jessica's and Ashley's experiences clearly demonstrate the difference between the 50:50 concept and the classic approach to college. With Ashley's classic approach she has focused 100% of her energy into academics and is likely waiting for either medical school or her first job to show her how the real world is going to be. Jessica on the other hand has taken an aggressive attitude towards her career and is finding out if being a doctor is right for her while in college, all while taking care of her grades. There is no doubt that Jessica is spending more time and energy on college than Ashley, but which student do you think is better off in the end?

Ultimately, the goal is to have enough information and experience to decide if you have picked the right career goal. What happens if you decide that you've picked the *wrong* career goal? Let's use Jessica and Ashley to look at this scenario. Let's assume both Jessica and Ashley have chosen their career goals of being doctors for the wrong reasons. In Ashley's situation, using the classic approach to college, she will likely not recognize what being a doctor is like until she's in medical school, which makes the realization that she made the wrong decision much later than it needs to be. For Jessica, who followed the 50:50 concept, her situation is similar, except she will realize much earlier than Ashley that she made the wrong choice. At first glance, the differences between these two situations may not seem very big, but you would be mistaken. For Ashley, once she recognizes she had made the wrong choice, she is no closer to finding what the *right* choice for her would be, and unless she has an unlimited supply of money, she will likely find herself in a very stressful dilemma between student loans and being lost as to what to do for a career. Jessica on the other hand, would likely recognize during college that she has made the wrong choice and has time on her side. Jessica now has the luxury of going through the process all over again. I know this may seem like a daunting task, but think about the timeframe that we're talking about. Jessica is focused on making the right choice that will set herself up for the rest of her life. When it's viewed from this perspective, a year or two spent focusing on finding out what the best career would be seems minor in the big picture. Jessica has a huge advantage over Ashley in not only knowing earlier that she has made the wrong choice, but also by having a strategy for what to do next: pick a new career goal and start figuring out if her new career goal is the right choice.

The 50:50 concept is designed so it can be applied to all fields of study, regardless of what interests you have. In the example of Jessica and Ashley the 50:50 concept was applied in the field of human medicine. Let's take a look at another example, in a completely different field and see how the concept can be used. Lauren was a college freshman and like most typical freshman, she had no idea what career to pursue. After going through the career goal exercise it was clear to her that her passion was dancing, but she was convinced she could never do it as a career. For Lauren the 50:50 concept made her recognize one major thing....she had based her decision that she couldn't pursue dancing as a career without ever getting good information. Lauren recognized she was making her decision on what "they" say. I always challenge my students about where they get information. Typically the answer is "you know, that's just what *they* say". **"They" is just another way of saying you have no idea where your information came from, which automatically makes it bad information.** Once Lauren recognized this, setting her career goal was easy....to be a phenomenal ballet dancer. Lauren's application of the 50:50 concept to decide whether she made the right decision or not was basically the same as Jessica's from the previous example, except tailored to Lauren's career goal. Lauren used the internet to find the best ballet companies in her area, which for her ended up being not very local (closest being in New York and Chicago), but since she could get a lot of information by email, this was not a dead end, but rather something she would just have to deal with. By writing professional emails with direct questions she was able to get good information from sources that had real-world experience. Questions such as these:

-Within the ballet discipline, what different careers can I pursue?
-What would my day-to-day life be like as a professional dancer?
-What are the major perks of being a professional dancer?
-What are the major downsides to being a professional dancer?
-What salary can I expect to make as a professional dancer?
-Is the cost of professional training worth it in the end?

By shadowing professional dancers and volunteering her time, Lauren can could gain all the information and real-world experience necessary to decide if she had chosen the right career goal, which is exactly what the 50:50 concept is designed to do.

The choice itself, on whether the career choice was right or not, was completely up to Lauren. **Making the decision of whether or not you have chosen the right career goal is not an easy decision, but one that absolutely needs to be made using good information only.**

I'm going to use Brandon as my final example and highlight a major pitfall some students fall into. Brandon, a college sophomore, has no idea what he wants to do for a career. Brandon went to college after high school, because... "Well...that's what you do after high school". After spending six months going through the career goal exercise he's still stuck with no clear career path jumping out at him as something he would like to do for a career based on the professors he's talked to. What should Brandon do next? Should he give up and go back to not having a strategy or a plan on what to do next? Instead of giving up, Brandon decides a different path, he questions if he has been talking to the right people. Brandon has always had a passion and talent for cooking, but has never thought of it as anything more than a hobby. **He was always convinced that the only way to get a good job was to go to a 4-year college and graduate, which is just plain wrong.** After getting good information he realizes that although he could graduate with a degree, he would be stuck in a job the rest of his life, instead of spending time on a career he would love. By having an aggressive attitude, Brandon set a career goal of being a kickass chef and jumped right into the 50:50 concept to check if he had made the right decision. He made contacts at the multiple culinary schools and asked these questions:

-What are the different cooking specialties I can go into?
-What would my day-to-day life be like as a chef?
-What are the major perks of being a chef?
-What are the major downsides to being a chef?
-What salary can I expect to make as a chef?
-Is the cost of going through culinary school worth it in the end?

Brandon knew he had made the right career goal choice within weeks, after getting good information from good sources and shadowing multiple chefs.

The example of Brandon highlights a major pitfall for some students and leads me to the last piece of advice on career goals: **don't limit yourself**. If the departments at your college don't point you in the right direction, look at other colleges that offer different programs. Don't limit yourself to careers that take a 4-year college degree. Trade schools are wonderful programs that fit very well for a lot of people. Careers in the culinary arts, aesthetics (beauty school), information technology, medical technology, veterinary technology, etc... are excellent choices. Remember this is a very personal choice;

you must be honest with yourself if you ever want to set yourself up for long-term success.

The "career" category of the 50:50 concept focuses on both gaining good information <u>and</u> getting real-world experience. You need both of these pieces in order to know if you've made the right decision. Good information comes from experts in the field and real-world experience comes from doing "career" activities, such as volunteering, interning, shadowing, interviewing, and working in the field. Once you are able to answer the six core questions <u>and</u> you have real-world experience from "career" activities, you will have everything you need to decide if you've made the right choice. All you need to do is follow your gut feel and make the decision. If you decide that you made the right pick, then the focus becomes figuring out the best way to obtain your goal. If you decide that you didn't pick the right career goal, you need to start back at Phase 1, set a new career goal and start figuring out if your new goal is the right one for you.

You will be ready to decide if you made the right choice when you know what your career will be like in the real world. Take an aggressive attitude toward answering your questions and don't rely on any single person for your answers; be sure to get information from at least three different professionals before making your decision. Lastly, do whatever it takes to get the real-world experience you need. Take the time early in your career to make sure you are in the right place, even if it means working for free. Ultimately, the choice is yours. With good information and real-world experience on your side you can be confident about your decision, no matter what that decision may be.

Setting a career goal is just one key point of the college strategy. Once the other two key points have been explained we will put the entire strategy together in the strategy planning chapter.

Chapter 2
Understanding the Word
"Choice"

In the game of basketball, having a strategic plan is only as good as the execution of that plan. In the game of college the same rules apply. Key Point 1 focused on setting up your strategic plan. In Key Points 2 & 3 we're going to focus on how to best execute the strategic plan you've made. Execution of your plan ultimately depends upon having the right mindset so you stay focused and driven toward your goal. The right mindset boils down to understanding two important things so you can best execute your strategy: understanding the word "choice" and personal responsibility.

In the game of basketball it's the coaches' job to make sure all their players understand their roles during the game and have the right mindset, but what about in the game of college? What's the proper mindset to have and who is supposed to help guide that mindset? **The proper mindset to have is called the <u>mature mindset</u> and in the game of college, to be successful, you need to be the coach and the player.** The mature mindset is a way of thinking which most people would say is the way adults *should* think. As we have discussed before, using the right terminology can make a huge difference. This is the reason I don't call this way of thinking "adult". Most people relate the word adult with an age, usually 18, and assume that once you reach that age you are now an adult. I think we can agree that just because you're 18 years old it doesn't mean you've changed the way you think about things. It's for this reason I came up with the term "mature mindset" to describe the way adults *should* think. I'm sure you can think of people well over the age of 18 that still think and act like a child, and on the flip side, you can probably think of people under the age of 18 that act like mature adults. Since age is obviously not an indicator of mindset, and the word adult is directly linked to an age, I only use the phrase "mature mindset" to describe the proper mindset to have to win at the game of college.

Let's take a minute and look at the difference between a child's mindset and a mature man's or woman's mindset, because what separates them are really only three major differences.

Differences Between a Child's and a Mature Man's or Woman's Mindset

Difference #1 – Long Term Thinking. A child only sees and understands the world directly in front of them. There is no understanding that the decisions made today can have long-term effects on the future.

Someone with a mature mindset, on the other hand, recognizes, understands, and takes into account the long-term effect their decisions will have. It's this difference that makes it impossible to successfully set career goals or understand the need for one if you have a child's mindset. It's my hope that the steps of Key Point #1 have given you a clear path to transition from a having a child's mindset to having a mature mindset, with regard to long-term thinking.

Difference #2 – Decision Making. A person with a mature mindset understands that everything that happens to him or her is based on personal choice. They also understand that information received from other people is nothing more than advice. A person with a child's mindset has the major decisions in their life made by other people (mainly their parents) and thinks there is no choice but to follow those decisions. It's this difference that makes it impossible for someone to take control of their own future. This is the main focus of Key Point #2 and will be addressed in detail in the rest of this chapter.

Difference #3 – Personal Responsibility. A person with a mature mindset takes personal responsibility for their decisions and actions (both good and bad), while someone with a child's mindset blames other people for what happens to them. Most people, regardless of their mindset, have little problem taking responsibility for the positive things that happen, but when their decisions lead to negative outcomes the difference between the mature mindset and a child's mindset becomes obvious. It's this difference that makes it impossible for someone with a child's mindset to learn from the past. This difference is directly linked with the difference in decision making, but is so important that it deserves special attention. This difference is the focus of Key Point #3.

As people get older and transition physically from being children to adults, it is assumed that their mindset will change as well, but this is typically not the case. For most people, the transition of their mindset lags way behind the transition of their bodies, as evidenced by the majority of students answering that they still see themselves as kids, not men or women. Through my experiences I have come to believe that there are only two ways people will change their mindset (or the term more commonly used: "grow up") and stop thinking and acting like a kid and transition into a mature mindset. Option 1: someone recognizes they are acting like a kid and chooses to start taking control of their own life and makes the choice to live with a mature mindset. Option 2: someone has a catastrophic event in their life that forces them to change their mindset, for example, a major car accident or death of someone very important. I hope your transition to a mature mindset happens by option 1 and not because of something catastrophic happening in your life. In this chapter we are going to focus on option 1 and what it takes to make this transition, which simply comes down to understanding the word "choice".

Making decisions when you have a mature mindset can be described in a six-word phrase: everything you do is your choice, or as you say it to yourself: EVERYTHING I DO IS MY CHOICE. When explaining this phrase for the first time I use a series of very blunt questions to make my point. For example, did someone hold a gun to your head and make you get out of bed this morning? Or go to class this afternoon? Or walk in my office and talk to me? The answer is of course no, but these questions show the raw level of understanding necessary to apply the phrase "everything I do is my choice". Once you understand this phrase at that raw level you will recognize that everything you do is choice: when you get out of bed, what you eat for breakfast, if you go to class, if you shower, what you do with your spare time, who you hang out with, who you don't hang out with, if you do your homework, if you go out at night, etc. Everything is choice....everything. I'm not saying there aren't consequences for your choices; there are, and that topic will be covered in Key Point #3, personal responsibility. This chapter is entirely focused on making sure you understand the word choice.

Understanding the word choice is the core of the mature mindset because without it you're leaving all the decisions that run your life to someone else, just like children do. Once this concept is understood it typically leads to a huge sense of empowerment, and with that comes a huge sense of responsibility. Typically, it's this sense of responsibility that makes people scared of truly embracing this concept. Simply put, it's just easier to be told what to do than to be responsible for making all the decisions in your life, and although I agree it's easier, it sets you up for long-term disappointment because you will not be doing what you truly want to do....you will be doing what someone else wants you to do. This transition is not easy, but necessary if you want to spend the rest of your life enjoying the passions that you have.

I can only assume that you are thinking to yourself that all this sounds great, but my parents are still so involved with my life that this idea isn't really possible. With a mature mindset how much your parents are involved in your decisions is your choice...not theirs. If your parents are helping you pay for college, this again, is your choice. All of your choices have consequences, some good and some bad, but ultimately it comes down to your choice.

To finish this section I want to share with you a trick that I personally use to help keep myself focused on the fact that everything I do is choice. Based on the majority of the conversations I hear around campus, I have come to realize that most people spend a large portion of their time complaining about how someone is screwing them over or wasting their time. Simply put, most people are wasting huge amounts of both time and energy complaining about other people. This is time and energy that could be used for constructive things, like researching what they want to do with the rest of their lives. I am guilty of doing this as well, and in order to stay focused I have posted all over my office, both inside and out "The rules of my office". These rules apply to everyone that enters my office, most of all me. There are 3 simple rules* that if followed nearly ensure that I stay focused on the fact that I'm in charge of what I do and that I take responsibility for the choices I make.

Rule 1: No whining.
Rule 2: No complaining.
Rule 3: No excuses.

The execution of any good strategic plan starts with good decision making, which is the direct product of a person's mindset. To succeed at college the right mindset to have is the mature mindset, which focuses on making good decisions through the simple principle of understanding that everything you do is your choice.

*I cannot take credit for the three rules. I learned this from a book about a great basketball coach, John Wooden.

Chapter 3
Personal Responsibility

Understanding the word choice and taking personal responsibility for all your decisions are directly linked, but these are completely separate issues that each deserves separate attention. Key Point #2 focused on decision making and understanding the word choice, and in this chapter we will focus on what happens after you make your decision and the consequences that follow.

All choices have consequences. When you have a mature mindset and you're the one making all the decisions, you must live with the consequences of those decisions. You must take personal responsibility for everything you do. This means that **when your decisions lead to good outcomes you get all the credit and when your decisions lead to bad outcomes you take all the blame.** No whining. No complaining. No excuses. As highlighted in Key Point #2 the focus needs to be on *how* you think about college, which really breaks down into transitioning your mindset away from the way children think and into the way mature adults think. When it comes to personal responsibility, people with a child's mindset typically have no problem taking credit when their decisions lead to positive things, but it's usually a different story when it leads to something negative. When I talk about personal responsibility and the need for it, I am talking about taking responsibility for every decision you make, both good and bad. Just like decision making can be summed up in six words, **personal responsibility can be summed up in nine words: you are 100% responsible for every decision you make or as you say it to yourself: I AM 100% RESPONSIBLE FOR EVERY DECISION I MAKE.**

When you have a mature mindset and take responsibility for all the choices you make, something really interesting starts to happen: you can learn from your decisions. I know that sounds simple and a bit cheesy, but think about it for a second. If every time you make a bad decision you choose to blame other people for what happened, you will never learn from your mistakes, because it was somebody else's fault. Only when you take full responsibility for what happens to you can you learn from the past and make better decisions in the future. Ever hear someone say the phrase "What doesn't kill you makes you stronger"? I hear this phrase and immediately think of personal responsibility, because I find this phrase to be true only if someone is willing to take responsibility for their choices and learn from them.

Being 100% responsible for your actions is not easy, but it's essential if you want to stop thinking and acting like a kid. **For those I have personally seen transition from blaming others to taking 100% responsibility for their decisions, I can**

64

sum up their transition in one word, <u>empowering</u>. They all feel empowered to pursue whatever they set out to accomplish. They no longer feel trapped or powerless in what happens to them, but instead become self-confident.

Taking responsibility for your choices is empowering, and with empowerment comes self-confidence. Most students in college have very little self-confidence, which in my opinion is a direct result of students having a child's mindset, not a mature mindset. When you don't view everything you do as choice and you don't take responsibility for every decision you make, everything bad that happens to you will always be someone else's fault. This mindset (a child's mindset) directly leads to low self-confidence because you're not taking responsibility for what you <u>choose</u> to do and therefore can't learn from your past decisions. **When you start to take charge of all the decisions you make and are willing to live with the consequences of those decisions, you will gain self-confidence, which is vital to staying focused and driven towards your career goal.**

As a grown man or woman with a mature mindset **you are 100% responsible for every decision you make and you know that everything you do is your choice.** By understanding these two phrases you will be in control of your own future, have self-confidence and the right attitude to accomplish the high career goals you've set for yourself.

Chapter 4
Strategy Planning

In the very beginning of this book I defined college success as having a career goal and a strategic plan to achieve that goal by the time you graduate. I can think of no game in the world, including the game of college, that someone can expect to win if they don't have a winning strategy in mind. So far in discussing the game of college we've turned the complicated question of what's the best winning strategy into manageable pieces that describe how to set a goal, what that goal should be (Key Point #1) and the mature attitude it takes to stay focused on obtaining that goal (Key Points #2 & 3). Now the only step left is to figure out the best way to make the pieces fit together.

What I've done is highlight six strategy-planning suggestions designed to help you keep the right perspective about your strategy and stay focused on the game you're playing so you can win, and enjoy your career instead of settling for a job.

Suggestion #1 - Professional Perspective

Perspective is defined as a particular attitude toward something or a point of view. How you view yourself is the single most important thing when it comes to putting your strategy into action. So what is the right perspective to have?

I strongly suggest that you never view yourself as a student. This is another situation where a certain word, in this case the word student, automatically makes you think a certain way because of your experience. Your entire life you've been a student, from kindergarten through high school, so using that same word to describe a new attitude and approach makes no sense; you're setting yourself up to be confused. My advise is this....**don't view yourself as a student, instead view yourself as an early professional that's not very good at your chosen profession**. This might sound strange, but once you think about the difference between these two perspectives it makes perfect sense. When you think of yourself as a student, what goal are you driven toward? For most the answer is graduation. When you think of yourself as someone that has chosen to do something you're not very good at, what goal are you driven toward? The answer is **you are driven toward getting better, no matter what it takes....and that's exactly the attitude you want to have**. If your career goal is to be a kick ass teacher you need to view yourself as a teacher...a teacher that's not very good at teaching yet. With this perspective you should view your college courses and every other "career" activity as something that's going to help you get better at your chosen profession.

Most things in this world are out of your control, but not everything. **You are in control of what you choose to do and how you view yourself**. By combining this professional perspective with the understanding of the terms choice and personal responsibility, you can use this control to your advantage. By making a little change in your perspective you can better improve your strategy on how to win at the game of college.

Suggestion #2 – Be a Nerd

Be a nerd - I'm not sure there's a better way to say it. Look at anyone that's chosen a career path and has been successful at obtaining their goals and I'll bet you they are a nerd. I am a huge nerd, no doubt about it, and I am proud of it. If you look up nerd in the dictionary it's defined as an intelligent expert in a particular discipline. How is that a bad thing?

I know in high school it's typically unpopular to enjoy studying or learning, but the game of high school is over. You are now playing a different game with different rules. One of the biggest problems I see on campus are students that genuinely have a passion for something, but hold back because they are stuck in the high school mindset where not caring about things makes them cool. As a professor I can tell you there is *nothing* better than to see a young professional passionate about *something*. I don't care what

69

the person's passion is, as long as there is passion for something. **There is no chance for you to be great at anything unless you have passion for something**. Be a nerd and follow your passion.

Suggestion #3 – Always Rely on Gut Feel

"To thine own self be true" is one of William Shakespeare's most quoted lines and it's for good reason. You know yourself better than anyone else. As you make your way through college and transition from a kid's mindset to a mature mindset always be true to yourself.

There are a lot of decisions for you to make as you start college and start to plan the rest of your life, like what career goal you should pick. When hard decisions need to be made, rely on two things: good information from credible sources and your gut feel. One of the biggest problems most people run into when making big decisions is over-thinking the situation. In my experience, most people know the right decision to make, but it's their self-doubt that gets in the way. My advice is trust yourself and let your gut feel tell you what choice to make. To thine own self be true.

Suggestion #4 – Privacy

Being honest with yourself is essential if you're ever going to trust your own gut feel. This is why for both phases of the career goal exercise, including the 50:50 concept, I strongly suggest you keep things private. Privacy is the only way you are ever going to be completely honest with yourself, and without honesty there is almost no chance of choosing the right career goal.

As discussed previously, lack of self-confidence is a very common issue for most college students. In particular, I've found it's especially common in students that never spend time with themselves. I know that might sound a little goofy, but how can you expect to know who you are if you've never spent time with yourself? It takes time, good questions, and honest answers to understand who you are and from this comes self-confidence. **Privacy is an essential part of gaining self-confidence**. You need to utilize your private life to be honest with yourself, and in turn this will give you self-confidence.

Suggestion #5 – Terminology

School is not college. It's a completely different game with different rules. You're also not a student, you're a young professional that's not very good at your profession (yet). Both student and school are words that you already know. This can easily confuse you in the game of college by assuming the same rules of high school apply. By simply using different words you can trick yourself into recognizing this is a different game. **Starting college assuming it's just like high school, but harder, is a very costly mistake** that happens too often. This simple trick is an easy way to help keep your mind on the right track so you never make this mistake.

Suggestion #6 – Be Aggressive

Don't be afraid to ask yourself the hard questions or make the hard choices that should be addressed when you're at college. Too often students choose not to address what they want to do with the rest of their lives because it's too complicated and they have no clear directions on where to start. As a result a lot of students graduate college with no better understanding of what career they want to pursue than when they started.

So far in this book we have discussed how to address the question of what career you want to pursue and I've provided direction on how to aggressively pursue the answers to your questions. Time goes really fast, and without an aggressive attitude towards answering your questions you will be relying on the hope that you will magically stumble onto something you will love to do the rest of your life. With something so valuable, it seems foolish to leave it up to chance. Remember, aside from sleep you will spend more time working than anything else the rest of your life. Be aggressive and be sure to use your energy wisely during college.

Suggestion #7 - Take Yourself Seriously

Are people really going to take you seriously if you follow the advice in this book? I mean, you're just a college kid right? WRONG. **You are a young professional with a mature mindset that's aggressively pursuing your career goal.**

You cannot expect anyone to take you seriously if you don't take yourself seriously. If you treat yourself like a kid, everyone around you will treat you like a kid. Again, this is not an age thing; I know 50-year-olds that act like kids and are treated like kids by everyone around them. The only way people will take you seriously is if you take yourself seriously. Those that don't take you seriously aren't going to help you, and you don't need to waste any more time or energy on them.

Unfortunately, there are no exercises you can do to help decide the best way to put what you've learned together. How you choose to put these pieces together is completely your choice. My advice is to take what you've learned and follow your gut feel. You know yourself better than anyone else. The advice I've given you and the exercises I've described in this book are not perfect, they are nothing more than information (good information from a trusted source...I hope). How you use them is 100% on you.

No matter what advice you get from this book or anyone else, in the end, the only thing that matters is what you choose to do. You cannot wait for people to give you what you want; if you want something you need to go get it yourself. Stay focused on picking the right career goal, making good choices based on good information, taking personal responsibility for your decisions, and be sure to enjoy the process. The strategy you choose to use in college is up to you. No matter what strategy you choose to use, I hope it's one that you have given thought to and not left up to chance. I can think of no game in the world that someone can expect to win if they don't have a winning strategy in mind.

Section 2
The Tools & Rules of the Game

Introduction

In any game there are specific tools you must use and rules you must follow if you're going to play the game properly. For example, in the game of basketball you must use a certain size basketball (tool) and know how the game is played (rules).

The game of college follows the same basic principle as any other game; there are specific tools that are used and rules that are followed if you're going to play the game properly. The big difference between the game of college and the game of basketball is that in the game of basketball there is a referee to stop someone that isn't properly following the rules. In the game of college, no such referee exists, so it's up to you to know the proper tools and rules of the game.

This section is designed to break down the basic tools and rules of the college game. These are the essential pieces that you will need to know and understand if you wish to win the game. Though each college is different, the tools and rules highlighted here are consistent and can be applied regardless of where you have chosen to go to college.

Chapter 5
Classes

There are two main types of courses offered in college: traditional and on-line courses. Both have their benefits and drawbacks. I am only going to discuss traditional courses because it's the only experience I have. I've never taken or taught an on-line course, which makes me a bad source of information for on-line courses. In this section we're going to focus on traditional classes and the tools and rules of an individual college class.

Most bachelor degrees require students to accumulate 120 hours of credit spread across a variety of courses with a focus on a particular area, your major, but with exposure to things outside of your major. These courses outside of your major are called general education credits or "gen ed's". The 120 total hours of courses are designed to give you enough detailed information in your major and give you a breadth of knowledge across multiple disciplines.

At first glance general education credits might seem kind of stupid. Why take a dance appreciation course if you are studying to be an electrical engineer? The answer is exposure. General education courses are designed to expose you to the world from different perspectives. I advise you to utilize these courses as an avenue for opening up your mind to a new a way of thinking. This does not mean that you are going to fall in love with dance and want to change majors, but it does give you another perspective on the world, and that's never a bad thing. You will get to see how dancers view the world.

You are likely going to need 120 credit hours to graduate...but what's a credit hour? A credit hour is *designed* to tell you how much time and energy should be spent on each course. Most students realize the number of credit hours for a particular course typically matches the number of hours spent in a single week in the classroom or lab. For example, for a 4-credit course you can expect to be on campus, in the classroom or lab, for 4 hours. What most students don't realize is that a credit hour can also be used as a gauge for how much time you should be spending out of the classroom for a particular course. The rule to follow is that for every 1-credit hour taken, you should be spending approximately 2 hours outside of class on that material. So if you are taking a 4-credit class that's 12 hours a week you should be spending on that course (4 in class and 8 outside).

Typically a full load of college courses is a minimum of 12 credit hours a semester. Based on the 2-1 system of looking at credit hours it works out that for a 12 credit semester you should be spending 36 hours a week on those classes. If you plan to graduate college in 4 years, without taking summer courses and no re-takes, you would have to take 15 credit hours a semester for 4 years. Based on the 2-1 system, if you take 15 credit hours a semester you should be spending 45 hours a week on course work alone. In the working world the number of hours to be considered full time is 40 hours a week. This is why **college, if approached properly, is the equivalent of full time job**. Now, not all courses are going to require 2 hours of time out of class per credit hour, and some are going to take more than that, but in general it will balance itself out. This is where understanding what courses you're going to take and how much time and energy go into each one can help you tremendously. Meeting with your advisor to discuss courses and using information from other students are valuable resources you should take advantage of. **As a general rule I advise you not to take more than 16 credit hours a semester.** Instead of trying to take as many courses as possible, view college as a 4-year business plan and focus on sticking to that plan. By following your plan you can graduate in 4 years and not be overwhelmed by taking too many credits in any single semester.

The first day of every new course you will be given a syllabus. **The syllabus is not just a piece of paper the professor puts together to help you understand what the semester is going to be like**. **You should treat a course syllabus like a contract between you and the professor**. On the syllabus should be a description of the course, the professor's office hours, contact information for the professor, what material will be covered, how you will be graded and at least a rough outline of when certain topics will be covered. Professors are given a lot of freedom to develop their own syllabus, but these key elements should always be present.

The syllabus gives you the first glimpse into what the professor expects from you throughout the semester. As I mentioned, you can view your syllabus like a contract between you and the professor, and only under special circumstances should that contract be changed. If the grading scale for the class is on the syllabus, you should not expect the professor to change the grading scale for any reason throughout the entire semester. If there is a statement on the syllabus that states no extra credit will be given, you should not expect there to be extra credit given. There is a luxury in getting this information the first day of class - it lets you know exactly what is expected of you and what the *rules* of the class are.

Just like every teacher you've ever had in the past, each professor is going to have his or her unique style and personality. In college you have the freedom to pick the courses you want to take, and at most colleges, there will be multiple professors teaching the same course, so you can also choose which professor to take. When choosing between multiple professors teaching the same course, you should treat it more like a business decision than a personal decision, because in the end, this has nothing to do with being friends with the professor. In other words, you should gather as much information as possible and use your gut feel. The only expectation you should have from your professor is professionalism, so don't be too quick to judge whether you like a professor because of the way they dress or the way they talk. You should judge them on how much they can teach you.

Books are a topic that I'm sure you have gotten advice on from others. As a professor my advice is simple. **Unless instructed otherwise wait until the first day of class to figure out what books you need to buy.** Professors change textbooks quite often, some don't use textbooks at all, and some use it as a supplement to their lectures. The only way to know is to wait and get the information directly from the professor. Books are expensive and with the outrageously low buy back prices that most college bookstores have, you'll want to be smart about how you spend your money. In the last couple of years there have been some new avenues for getting and using books for college classes that you should be aware of. First, most college libraries have book holdings for most large courses taught on campus. What this means is that most textbooks are available in the college library for students to use. Typically you are not allowed to check them out and take them home, but you can use them within the library for a set amount of time (typically 2-4 hours). This is a great way to save money and not hinder your performance in class, if the textbook is not used

83

extensively throughout the semester. Another good avenue for textbooks are websites that rent used textbooks, instead of the traditional buy and sell back model that has been used for years. I've personally never rented a textbook, but I have gotten very good feedback from former students.

Lastly, I want to discuss the issue of procrastination. A semester is approximately 4 months long (a quarter = 2 ½ months). **Probably the most common problem, especially with freshman, is a lack of basic understanding that a semester is 4 months long**. When I teach a course, each exam is worth an equal amount of points throughout the entire semester and I never give extra credit. If a student gets behind early in the semester, it is nearly impossible for them to make up the ground they've lost. Approach each class as a 4-month business deal and be sure to work just as hard at the beginning as you do in the end. **Unlike high school, college professors are not going to pass you just because you came to class and turned in your homework. You must earn the grades you get in college and in order to get good grades you need to perform well throughout the entire semester.** Procrastination is a real problem for a lot of students because it worked so well in high school. High school is over, and in the game of college procrastination can cause you nothing but problems.

I constantly hear students say: "I work better under pressure" or "I'm at my best when my back is against the wall". The problem with these attitudes in the college game is that if you wait for the stress to build and for your back to be against the wall, most of the time it's too late. There has *never* been a semester that I haven't had *at least* a dozen good, smart students beg for extra credit to make up for work they slacked off on early in the semester. I never have nor will I ever give them extra credit. I know this may seem harsh or mean, but think about it from the professor's perspective. All the rules were clearly laid out the first day of class and they chose not to play by them. You need to **approach each semester as a 4-month business deal, and be on your game from the beginning to the end of the semester**. Find ways to stay motivated throughout the entire course. If you can stay motivated on your own, that's great; if you need the help of friends or family, that's great too. Do whatever it takes. One trick I used when going through college to stay focused and motivated was what I now call the cost/benefit trick.

Cost/Benefit Trick

Every semester look at your tuition bill or call the University Bursar's office (the place where you send your money) and ask what a single credit hour of tuition cost. It will be different if you are in-state versus out-of-state, so be prepared to tell them which one you're looking for. Then take the syllabus and add up the total number of times you are going to meet in the classroom or lab throughout the entire semester. For example, if you are taking a 4-credit Biology class from Dr. Brown that meets every Monday, Wednesday and Friday and lab meets once a week on Thursday afternoons, then look at a calendar and add up the number of total times you will meet. Let's say in Dr. Brown's class there will be 38 individual meeting times for the course. Take the cost of an individual credit hour (let's say $400 /credit hour) and get the total cost of the course: $400 per credit hour X 4 credits = $1,600. Last, calculate how much each class is worth in real money: $1,600 / 38 = $42.10. This can work as a really good incentive not to miss class. This trick helped me put into context exactly why I was getting up to go to class, it made me realize that every time I didn't go to class I was wasting $42.10 of my own money. This trick isn't for everyone, but it helped me connect the college experience with my wallet and understand exactly how I was spending my money. This also helped me in picking the best courses to help me achieve my career goal, rather than just picking courses that best fit my schedule. It helped me realize that a good 8:00 AM course was worth getting up for if I knew I would get more out of it.

Chapter 6
Studying & Exams

Having good study techniques will directly lead to good exam scores, and the key to having good study techniques is understanding that your mind is unique. No one else thinks like you do, no one else has gone through the same experiences you've gone through, and because of this, no one is going to learn the same way you do. By understanding the strengths you have and utilizing them to your advantage, you can develop the best study techniques for yourself and use those techniques to score well on your exams, no matter what kind of exam you are taking.

The single most important principle that must be followed if you want a good study technique is repetition. Think about your favorite nursery rhyme from when you were a little kid. I'll bet you could sing that right now, even if you haven't heard it in 10 years. How are you able to do that? An even better question is how do you learn a new song that you really like? The answer is repetition. You listen to it over and over again, learning the chorus first, and then you learn the verses last. Repetition is the foundation for learning any new song and for the exact same reason; it's also the foundation of all good study techniques.

Good study techniques require that you see the material over and over again for a long period of time in order to retain the material. Most students that read this sentence completely agree with it, yet a lot of students still have bad study techniques. How can this be? The answer boils down to two misunderstandings: what is the best way to "see the material"? And what is a "long period of time"? Let's address each one of these separately.

In order to best "see the material" you first need to understand that you are unique. I know this may sound a bit more like a psychology lesson than advice on studying, but it's not. Your study techniques must be specifically tailored to you. You want to use the way your mind naturally works to your advantage. Too often I see students struggling to use a study technique that isn't good for them simply because they don't know other techniques exist. **My advice for picking the right study technique is to use good old fashion trial-and-error**. Try multiple techniques and then decide which one works best for you. Just because a certain technique works for someone else does not mean it will work for you. Don't forget, you're unique. Here is a list of study techniques to try.

Examples of Different Study Techniques

Game Time Study Technique – This is a technique that I have developed and seen enormous success from students that have used it. The details of this technique are described at the end of this chapter.

Note Cards – With this technique you want to translate the information given from your professor onto note cards. This technique is best used if you write a single word, phrase, or question on one side of a note card and the answer or definition on the other side. This technique is good for self-quizzing and memorizing clearly defined terms.

Acronyms – This technique works best with material that is made of multiple parts that you need to remember. For example, if you needed to learn the colors of the rainbow in order: red, orange, yellow, green, blue, indigo, and violet. With this technique you make an acronym that you can remember using the first letter of each color like: **R**yan's **O**verweight **Y**ellow **G**erbil **B**arked **I**nsults **V**iolently. These acronyms don't need to make sense to anyone but you, so use words and phrases you'll remember. When I was in college, one of the study groups I was in would have dirty acronym contests for the hardest material. Each member of the group would make an acronym for the same material and whichever acronym was the funniest we would use to study with. I can remember laughing out loud during exams...while writing the right answers and acing the exams.

Study Groups – Study groups are good to use because everyone is unique and brings a different level of understanding to the group. It allows you to ask questions and have the answers explained in different ways. A collection of good minds is better than any single individual.

Re-Teach Method – This technique is based on the idea that you really don't know material until you can teach it to someone else. If you can teach the material you've learned in class to a study group, then you know the material you're studying. You can also use family or friends with this technique if a study group isn't your style.

Re-Write Method – This technique focuses on the repetition of written notes. By re-writing the same set of notes over and over again it puts the material across your mind multiple times and forces you to think about each of the points you are re-writing.

Draw Pictures – A picture is worth a thousand words, and that's especially true when talking about class notes. Being able to understand material in a way other than written words is a great way to know if you understand material. Plus, you can use a picture as a reminder of important information during an exam. Don't be afraid to be creative. Just like using acronyms, the more personal you make the pictures, the easier it's going to be for you to remember. In other words, you don't have to use the pictures your professor uses during lecture if you can come up with something better.

Use Colors – This is more of a trick than a technique. Some minds work in colors; if you are one of these people you should use this to your advantage. Why work only with black or blue pens if your mind works in color. I suggest using colored pencils on both your notes and the exams (with your professors' permission) if it helps you remember material. Most good professors are going to be more concerned with you knowing the answer to the question then whether or not you used a pink or green pencil. Be sure to be courteous though and ask before using them on an exam. If this is the natural way your mind works, use it to your advantage.

The second misunderstanding in the sentence "Good study techniques require that you see the material over and over again for a long period of time in order to retain the material" is the phrase "long period of time". Would you be able to learn the lyrics of a new song if you listened to it for one hour straight? How about two hours? If you haven't guessed, I'm talking about the issue of cramming. **Cramming is by far the most common study mistake made and is the easiest one to fix**. By cramming the night before, or even two nights before an exam you are trying to learn weeks' worth of information in hours, which leads to two big problems. First, you've left yourself no time to ask questions if you don't understand the material you are studying. Second, assuming you were able to pull off a good exam grade, you have almost no chance of remembering, long-term, the material you studied. Cramming, at best, lets you short-term memorize what you've studied, with almost no chance for long-term storage of information. Next in this section I will discuss the implications of short-term versus long-term learning, but we still need to answer the question of what is meant by a long period of time. **I advise that you should start studying no later than 2 weeks before each exam**. With multiple classes, each with multiple exams throughout the semester, the only sensible approach to this is to buy a calendar and the first week of classes write down each exam date and make study times for each. Be aware that you will often have multiple exams in different classes during the same week, so have a study schedule figured out and give yourself enough time for each class.

How much do you remember from your classes in high school? Most high school students remember very little from the classes they took....I know, I teach freshman courses. The issue at hand is why don't most graduating high school students remember much? The answer goes back to the issue we discussed during the strategy section of this book describing goals and how hard people work towards them. People typically work just hard enough to get what they want and nothing more. The goal of most high school students, that want to go to college, is to graduate with a high enough grade point to get into the college they want to go to. So with all the focus on graduation, students will work just hard enough to get it. Most high school students aren't interested in learning the material they're studying; they are interested in the grade. In college, if your only goal is to graduate, you're only going to work hard enough to get the grades you need so you can get a job. This will lead to the same result that happened in high school - you not remembering much from the classes you take. For those with a career goal in mind this is an absolute killer. There is no way you can be kick ass at anything without retaining the knowledge that you've learned. **If you set a high career goal, graduation should not be the goal you are working towards and getting good grades should not be the driving force behind learning**.

The cramming study techniques used by most high school students worked great in high school because most students know the system won't let them fail, so there is no reason to actually learn the material. For students that approach college the same way as they did high school, they will use the same techniques that got them good grades in high school, except now they can fail. Most students need a change in their study techniques early in their college career if they want to pass their courses. If you understand that college is a completely different game from high school and understand that the study techniques that worked for you in high school may not work in college, you will be well prepared for success on campus.

When trying different study techniques, you must be aware that change doesn't happen overnight - it takes time. The advice I give students who are struggling with making changes in their study techniques is to **view your mind as just another muscle**. Anyone that has ever exercised knows that when you're out of shape and need to get into shape the first two weeks absolutely suck, and then it gets much easier after you are over the two-week hump. This is exactly how the human mind works when it's out of studying shape or you're changing your techniques. Your mind, just like any other muscle in your body, needs to get comfortable with the changes that are happening and it takes about two weeks before you're going to feel comfortable. By understanding that your mind is just another muscle, you can approach studying problems the same way you would approach getting your body into shape and not freak out when the first two weeks are really hard. **Give**

the changes you're making at least two weeks before deciding if they've worked or not.

The last topic that needs to be covered in this section is cheating. This can be a major issue for those that view college the same as high school. The consequences for cheating at the college level are much more severe and can stay with you for a long time. Professors know how most high school students study and get through high school. In the new game of college you are 100% personally responsible for what you do and will be held accountable for your decisions. This is not meant to be a scare tactic; it's simply the truth. Cheating is taken very seriously and is not something you should take lightly in college.

Game Time Study Technique

As a professor I've seen a lot of very smart students get very bad grades on exams because of poor study habits. It's because of this I have developed the Game Time Study Technique. For the students I've worked with that understand and use it properly I've seen tremendous success.

The best way to explain the concept of the Game Time Study Technique is by using a hypothetical scenario. Let's pretend you are a good basketball player, and the big game is exactly six months away. Over the next six months, however, you and your team are not allowed to play basketball. You're not allowed to shoot a basketball, pass a basketball, or even touch a basketball. Instead, you are only allowed to play tennis. You can play as much tennis as you like in order to prepare for the basketball game, but no practicing basketball.

If you and your team spend six months practicing tennis everyday, could you be in good athletic shape by playing tennis only? Yes, tennis can put you in great overall physical shape. Will you be in good basketball shape? No. The only way to be in good basketball shape is to practice basketball. This scenario highlights exactly what goes on in most college classrooms and the problem that a lot of students face when it comes to studying for exams. An exam is the same as the big game, and studying is how you practice to get ready for the game. Most students that struggle on college exams aren't practicing for what the actual game is going to be like. Basically, they are playing tennis to get ready for a basketball game. I'll use an example from one of my own classes to demonstrate what typically happens in the classroom.

The exams I give in my courses are typically the only points students earn throughout an entire semester. My exams are always short answer or fill in the blank type questions, no essay and no multiple choice. What most students do is practice going over the material either by reading over the notes they've taken or by making note cards and reviewing them multiple times before the exam. Then, when the exam time comes they have to write their answers on paper, which is not the way they studied. For those that do poorly the same problem usually arises...they know the material but when it came to writing it down they draw a blank and can't come up with the answer. I know it's not that the students aren't studying, because when I ask them to answer questions verbally, they have no problem answering correctly. If you think about the exam as a game, and studying as practice, it starts to make sense...these students aren't practicing for the game they're about to play. They might be in exam shape, but not short answer and fill in the blank exam shape. It's the equivalent of someone practicing tennis to prepare for a basketball game.

The Game Time Study Technique focuses on preparing for the game exactly as it's going to be played. To best prepare for the game of basketball, you need to practice the game of basketball, as it will be played during the game. You practice this way so there won't be any surprises during the game that you haven't already practiced. This is the exact principle that the Game Time Study Technique follows for studying. Again, the exam is the game and studying is practice. Every professor will give multiple exams throughout a semester; with almost no exceptions all of the exams will follow the same format (in my case, all my exams are short answer or fill in the blank). You need to use this information to your advantage and practice answering questions exactly like you are going to answer them on the test. The key to using this method is writing and answering questions that are as close to the exam questions as possible. The best way to go about this is to use all your previous exams to learn from. Typically when a professor hands exams back, students are only interested in what they got wrong; this is a huge mistake. You need to pay very close attention to the <u>way</u> the professor asks exam questions, because this is how they are going to ask questions on the next exam, and the next exam, and the next exam. This is why first exams should always be the most difficult (unless you are given a practice exam), because you don't have a *real* idea of how your professor is going to ask questions.

Every exam you take is going to cover a set amount of material. If you know the types of questions that are going to be asked and you have previous exams to learn how the professor likes to write questions, there is nothing stopping you from basically writing your own practice exam before the real thing. This is practicing the game exactly like it's about to be played. After each exam you take you should be getting better at writing questions because you're learning from each exam you've already taken.

One key point to this technique that cannot be overlooked is the importance of answering the questions you write. In the example I used from my class I mentioned the problem of students freezing up when it came time to writing the answers down on paper, even though they knew the answer in their heads. Just like in basketball if you want to improve your jump shot, you need to practice your jump shot over and over again. If you know you freeze up when it comes to writing down answers on exams, you need to practice writing down answers over and over again, so during the exam it won't be a problem.

I have seen this technique work for everyone that has put it into practice. This technique is completely flexible to any type of exam. For example, if you are studying for a course where the professor asks multiple choice questions only, you should be writing multiple choice questions that you think might be on the exam, and that includes the wrong answers as well.

Remember, professors write exams using the same material they present in class. Try to figure out *how* the professor is going to ask questions and study exactly like the exam is going to be.

Chapter 7
Grades

In college your grades will be used as an indicator of how well you understand the course material and will be used to compare you to other students. Anyone that tells you that grades aren't important is lying to you. Grades are important, not the most important thing, but nevertheless important. As I have brought up many times in this book, the most important thing is to set a high career goal. Focus on achieving your career goal, have good study techniques, and good grades will follow.

One important point about grades that you must be aware of is the calculation of your grade point average (GPA) and the importance of how timing can make or break your GPA. The most common grading scale used in college is the 4-point grading scale. On the 4-point scale an A is worth 4.0 points, a B = 3.0, C = 2.0, and a D = 1.0. Some colleges will also give partial points such as a 3.5 or a 3.25, but not all, so be sure to know how your college grading system works from the very beginning so you have the best information possible.

The percentage of points you need to earn in any course to get your grade is completely up to the professor and should be clearly written on the syllabus. For each course you take you will be assigned a grade that then gets converted into a certain number of grade points, which is used to calculate your GPA. For example, if you were to get a B in your 4 credit hour freshman economics class, your B would be the equivalent of a 3.0. You would then multiply the number of credit hours for that class, 4, times the 3.0 that you earned, giving you a total of 12 grade points for that course. Do this for every class you take: add up the total grade points that you've earned, divide by the total number of credit hours taken and you will have your GPA.

Let's look at an example. Listed below are the courses that Jenny has taken in her first semester of her freshman year and the grades she's earned.

Class Taken (credits)	Grade Earned	Grade Point Equivalent	Total Grade Points Earned
Math 101 (4)	B	3.0	12
English 101 (4)	C+	2.5	10
Accounting 101 (4)	B	3.0	12
Freshman Seminar (3)	A	4.0	12

Total # of credits taken this semester= 15
Total grade points earned this semester= 46
(46 /15 = 3.06667)
GPA for this semester = 3.06667
Overall GPA = 3.06667

Jenny has taken 15 total credits and has earned a GPA of 3.07 during her first semester at college. This basic calculation of a GPA can be applied at any college as long as you know how your college converts grades to grade points.

Timing is a vital issue in your GPA calculation that you need to understand early in your college years, so it doesn't cause you problems. I'll be honest; most students who start college directly after finishing high school do poorly in the classroom their first couple of semesters. This is mostly due to the huge transition in their lives that comes with going to college. Some students have poor study techniques, some have a difficult transition living on their own, but mostly, it's because they view college as high school, only harder. For whatever reason, this poor performance in the first couple of semesters has much larger implications than most students realize. The real issue with this situation is the difficulty that comes with trying to bring your GPA up after you have accumulated a large number of total credit hours. **The more total credit hours you have the more difficult it is to change your overall GPA, so starting off the first couple of semesters with a high GPA is essential to graduating with a high GPA**. The attitude of "I can make it up later" simply won't work. Let's take a look at Jenny again, except now she's a senior with an overall GPA of 2.70. She is planning to graduate in one semester and desperately wants to get her GPA over a

3.0 so she can meet the minimum requirements for graduate school. She's already taken 105 total credits, has earned 283.5 total grade points, and is taking 15 credits her last semester so she can meet the 120 credit hour requirement for graduation.

Current GPA = 2.70
Total number of credits taken so far: 105
Total number of grade points earned: 283.5

Class Taken (credits)	Grade Earned	Grade Point Equivalent	Total Grade Points Earned
Microbiology (4)	A	4.0	16
Genetics (4)	A	4.0	16
Biotechnology (4)	A	4.0	16
Spanish IV (3)	A	4.0	12

Total # of credits taken this semester = 15
Total grade points earned this semester = 60
(60 /15 = 4.0)
GPA for this semester = 4.0

Overall GPA = (Total # of grade points earned) / (Total # of credit hours taken)
(283.5 + 60) / (105 + 15)
Overall GPA = 2.8625

Even though Jenny got a perfect 4.0 for her last semester, she was only able to bring up her overall GPA 0.1625 points. Because Jenny had so many total credit hours before starting her last semester the effect on her overall GPA was minor. The example of Jenny is a classic case of someone who tried to make up for her early mistakes in the classroom. Unfortunately her case is not special. **The first 2-3 semesters in college can make or break the overall GPA that you are going to graduate with**. By understanding how this calculation works and thinking about college as a 4-year business deal, you can easily avoid this issue and focus on classes right away, instead of digging yourself into a hole that you can't get out of.

My last point on grades has to do with terminology. Throughout this entire book you may have recognized that I always talk about the grades that you earn. This is another example of how a simple switch in the words you use can have a huge impact. Typically, I hear students talk about the grades their professor *gave* them. By thinking that professors give you grades, you are <u>not</u> taking personal responsibility. As a professor, I can honestly tell you that I have never given anyone a grade; students earn the grades they receive. My advice is that you only use the word *earn* when talking about the grades you receive. This forces you to take personal responsibility instead of blaming the professor or someone else for your grades. Remember, those who have a kid's mindset blame others, people with a mature mindset take personal responsibility.

Chapter 8
Scheduling & Choosing a Major

Most people will tell you that picking the right major is the most important decision you'll make at college, and by now you'll know I disagree. Picking the right career goal is much more important. **Picking the right courses and declaring the right major are both decisions that should be made based on your career goal.** It would be a mistake to mix up the order of the last sentence and plan your career goal because of the major you've declared. The best approach to take when thinking about what major to declare and classes to take is to think about them as stepping stones to get you closer to your career goal. In this section I'm going to show you the three most common approaches to picking a major. I am not going to cover topics like the best way to register for classes or how to fill out the right paperwork for declaring a major. Each of these topics will be covered in detail during your college orientation and can be found at any time by asking someone in the student affairs office at your college.

When it comes to declaring a major and picking classes students typically use one of these three approaches:

Approach #1 – The Lifestyle Approach. The lifestyle approach to declaring a major and picking classes is based entirely on the lifestyle someone wants to have while in college. The most important thing when using this approach is your current lifestyle, no class is more important than that. The most typical forms of this approach will have students saying things like *"There is no way I am taking 8:00 AM classes"* or *"I'm only interested in taking easy professors"*. With this approach there is no thought given to what career goal you're trying to pursue or even what major best suits your interests. One of the main reasons why students use this approach is because they are waiting for their classes to show them what they want to do with the rest of their lives. They figure if they take enough classes, somehow, they will stumble onto the perfect path. Unfortunately, as we have discussed throughout this book, that rarely happens. This approach is used more often than you'd think and should be absolutely avoided.

Approach #2 – The Academic Only Approach. The academic only approach to declaring a major and picking classes is based on the thinking that college is 100% about what happens in the classroom. If you relate this to the 50:50 concept, this group of people focuses 100% of their energy on "academics" with no energy focused on "career". Someone utilizing this approach typically makes decisions using bad and/or not enough information. Typically, student decisions on which major they declare are influenced by how much money they can make, knowing someone else in that major, or knowing someone that has a career in that field and likes it. With this approach there are no plans or attempts to see what a career in that field would be like in the real world. This is by far the most common approach taken in college and although it's better than the lifestyle approach, this too should be avoided.

Approach #3 – The Career Goal Approach. The career goal approach to declaring a major and picking classes is based entirely on your career goal. All choices and decisions are made with the attitude that you are a professional that's not very good at your chosen profession, so that you can focus on getting better. You want to take classes taught by professors that can help you the most. You rely only on good information from informed sources to make your decisions. For example, don't listen to your lazy roommate who never goes to class about what professors to take. With this third approach it's very well understood that you may change your major if you change your career goal after figuring out how the real world works. This approach fits perfectly into the 50:50 concept and should be utilized as early as possible in your college career.

If you have a high career goal and are focused on obtaining that goal, then declaring the right major and scheduling the right classes will not be an issue for you. You have 120 credit hours that you need to get in order to graduate, and you should have a strategy for maximizing those 120 credits. Be sure to utilize your academic advisors to make the best strategy. They are valuable resources and a good source of information. I advise that you set up regular meetings with your advisor no less than once a semester to discuss your strategy and make sure all the necessary paperwork is in order.

Chapter 9
Study Abroad

I have been very fortunate in my life to participate in study abroad programs both as a student and a professor and can say, without hesitation, that study abroad is one of the best things you can do during your college years. It's an experience that will teach you more than you could ever imagine or expect....and I'm not talking about the class material you'll be taught.

When I was a junior at Michigan State University I went to the Bahamas for about three weeks to study tropical biology. When I first signed up, I figured it was going to be three weeks of sun tanning, SCUBA diving and an easy way to get six credits. This was not the case. This was no vacation, but in the end I gained more than I ever thought I would. Although I learned a ton about tropical fish and coral, the most valuable thing I learned from this experience was a different viewpoint on the world. Most people in the United States think they understand the culture they live in extremely well. In my opinion, unless you view the US culture from another perspective, there is no way you can have a true understanding of it. No classroom or museum can give you that perspective; the only thing that can is cultural experience. I have also had the pleasure of teaching as a study abroad professor and have witnessed growth and development in my students that is unlike the students in my classrooms. **Study abroad is the single greatest opportunity to gain life experience in college**.

My advice for you is simple...GO! Pick a place in the world you have always read about or been fascinated with and make it happen. Nearly all colleges have people on campus that organize study abroad programs all over the world. Find out who does this at your college and set up a meeting to tell them you're interested. No matter what level of understanding you have of the programs offered the best way to get information is directly from the people who organize the programs.

If you make the decision to study abroad, I have some advice on how you should approach this opportunity (based on awkward experiences I've seen overseas that can easily be avoided):

- You should spend as much time as possible trying to understand the culture of the country you're going to. Learn what that culture thinks is rude, what the people dress like, and what type of food they eat.

- Do not go on a study abroad program if your plan is to use it as a vacation; this experience is not designed to be a vacation. It's designed to expose you to how other people in the world live.

- If the plan is to go with a group of students you already know, I would strongly advise you spend the majority of time alone or with only one other person in your program. When large groups travel together it's very easy to stay in the comfort of the group. If you are in a different culture you *should* feel like an outsider, this is not a bad thing. What you need to do is embrace that feeling and learn about the culture you are in....that's the main reason to study abroad.

- Try to immerse yourself in the culture that surrounds you; try to understand how people in that country spend their time so you can compare it to yours.

College is the time to open your mind to new ideas and experience things on your own maybe for the first time. In my experience study abroad can help you more than any other single thing you can do in college. I am a big believer in the study abroad experience and strongly encourage you to take advantage of study abroad opportunities during college.

Chapter 10
Free Time

Free time at college can be both a blessing and a curse. You want to make sure you balance the professional side of why you're in college with fun. The majority of this book has been focused on the career and academic issues of college, but having fun is a large part of the game, too. College campuses offer a wide variety of clubs and activities to fit just about every type of person and hobby. My advice is to buy a good calendar and make sure all the important time commitments for each semester are written down first. You need to be able to balance classes, studying, the "career" portion of the 50:50 concept, fun, and then the rest of life. Time management is the key to finding a good balance. Stay true to the commitments most important to you and fill the rest with fun.

Section 3
The Major Players in the Game

Introduction

In the game of basketball you need multiple groups of people in order to play the game properly. You need two different teams of five players and referees; additionally there are typically non-essential groups like coaches, bench players, fans, pep bands and cheerleaders. Each of these groups play a role in how the game will ultimately be played. Let's examine the relationships of a single player, the point guard. The point guard has many different relationships with those around him or her. Their relationship with the coach is going to be different from their relationship with their teammate, which is going to be different from their relationship with the fans. Just like in basketball, the same is true for the game of college. Think about all the relationships you currently have or are going to have in college: professors, new college friends, old high school friends, those high school friends that go to the same school as you, classmates, parents, advisors. Each group of people is different and your relationship with each group is going to be different as well. In this section I'm going to introduce the major groups of people that will influence you the most (the other players in the game) and discuss how understanding your relationships with these groups can make a huge difference during your time at college.

Typically, a student starting college can classify every relationship they have into one of three categories:

Category 1 – Family. This is pretty self-explanatory and encompasses everyone from your siblings to your parents to your favorite uncle who is proud of you for going to college.

Category 2 – Friends. This category is filled with people that you rely on to be there for you through thick and thin and to have fun with.

Category 3 – Strangers. This category is not only for all those people you don't know, but also for those people that are simply acquaintances. You may know these people by name or face, but don't *really* know who they are or anything about them.

Likely all your relationships currently fit into one of these categories, but once you start college you need to know there is a 4th category of relationship – professional.

Category 4 – Professional. This category is for people in your life that are solely focused on your professional development.

Although most family and friends are also interested in your professional development, there is a key difference that gives the professional relationship its own category, the term <u>unconditional</u>. What separates the professional relationship from family and friends is what I call the "give me a hug and make everything alright factor" or unconditional acceptance (some may call this unconditional love). Most students when entering college believe that no matter what they do wrong, they can fix the problem by saying sorry and asking for a second chance. When dealing with a true professional relationship saying sorry and expecting things to go back to normal won't work. Your success in college and in your career is dependent upon your understanding of how to act in a professional relationship. You need to be able to understand the difference between each category and have a strategy for how you handle each type of relationship, because each one is different and should not be handled the same.

Chapter 11
Professors

Professors are going to play a vital role in your life during college, and your relationship with them is going to be different than any other relationship you have. Their role in your life depends on how well you understand *how* professors think. You need to understand *how* professors view their students or there is no chance you're going to have a good relationship with them. By recognizing that professors belong in a new category of relationships, professional, you won't make the common mistake of interacting with your professors as if they are your family or friends. In this section I'm going to explain how professors think about students, what you can expect from your professors, the best way to communicate with them, and what they expect from you.

For someone just starting college, your professors are likely the first people you're going to interact with that fall into the professional relationship category, as described in the introduction of this section. **Not recognizing that professors belong in the professional relationship category, or even worse, not knowing the professional category exists, are the main causes for student problems with professors**. Most beginning students think professors are like every other teacher they've had, and expect the relationship to be the same as well, which is a mistake. Professors are not like every other teacher you've had, they're different. To remember they're different, **I suggest you only use the word professor, not teacher, for the instructors you have during college**. Just like substituting the word college for school, the same principle applies for the words professor and teacher.

Think about your four years of high school. I'm going to guess that in most of your classes you <u>knew</u> that no matter what you did you were going to pass. I'll even go a step further than that and guess that for most tests you were told exactly what you needed to study and how to answer each question before the test was given. I'm also going to guess that you got good grades but rarely felt pushed or challenged. How good are my guesses? If my guesses are close, let me tell you that you're not alone. **When you leave the game of high school and start the game of college, you must be aware that the rules of the game are different and that the rules that teachers played by in high school are not the rules that professors play by in college.** If you can understand that professors are not teachers, and that your relationships with them fall under a different category, with different rules, you are going to be able to see your professors as resources for good information, rather than teachers that are giving you grades.

Professors are <u>not</u> scary people who intend to "weed out" the bad students and make your life a living hell. Professors have one goal when you are taking their course.....to teach you material that will make you better professionally. Personally, as a professor, when someone asks me for advice, whether it's a student taking my course or a student I work with one-on-one, I always ask myself the same question before I answer....what's going to be best for this student 20 years from now? **Professors are not interested in being friends with you; they're interested in your professional development.** This is *how* professors think and *how* they approach students in their classes. **There is no pressure put on professors to make you pass, that's your personal responsibility, which is vastly different from the way high school was.** If you aren't willing to help yourself, you should not expect a professor to help you. This is not high school; this is college, and professors are different than teachers.

When I first started college, I was convinced that professors were mean, that they were out to get the students in their classes, and that they got pleasure out of seeing how many students they could fail out of one class. What I later realized was that the problem wasn't with my professors, but with my understanding of how the professor-student relationship works. If you go to your classes and think of your professors the same way you thought of your high school teachers (like I did the first couple years of college); you're going to struggle. I'll use the example of Kim and Kyle to highlight my point. Imagine two people, Kim and Kyle, on the playground playing a game of one-on-one basketball, first one to score 21 points wins. They start playing and each is keeping score separately <u>without</u> saying it out loud after each basket. Kyle is counting each basket as one point and Kim is counting each basket as two points. What's going to happen sometime during this game? Although it's a silly example it's exactly the same thing that goes on in most college classrooms. Professor and students are both in the same class-room, but there are two different sets of rules being used. If both aren't on the same page, there's going to be confusion and frustration sometime during the semester. Once you recognize *how* professors think you can start to understand why their policies exist....to make you better professionally. Believe it or not, policies such as not accepting late work, not grading on a curve, not taking any excuses, and failing those students that don't demonstrate an understanding of the material are actually in place to make you a better professional.

It's my hope that by explaining to you how professors think, you will better understand what a professional relationship is like. As I mentioned before, this is probably the first time you're going to have someone in your life that fits into this category of relationship and actually treats you professionally.

If you don't take yourself seriously as a professional, you can't expect a professor to take you seriously either. This is why having the attitude that you are a young professional with a mature mindset aggressively pursuing your career goal is better than any another approach. Not only does it keep you motivated, it sets you up perfectly to interact with the best resource you have on campus, your professors.

I want to highlight some key points and briefly discuss how you can better interact with your professors.

Professionalism

Professors are an excellent resource, not only for information, but also for career contacts, internships, and job openings. How you act each and every time you are around professors leaves an impression. You cannot expect anyone to take you seriously if you don't take yourself seriously (you will hear this theme continually repeated in this book for a reason). Act professionally and you will be treated professionally.

Most professors work hard at preparing their lectures and take their jobs very seriously. Be very cautious about the use of cell phones, iPods, laptops, etc., during classes. Most professors, myself included, feel that it is quite offensive to see students engaged in other things during class time. Imagine a conversation where the person you're talking to is checking their phone while you're trying to talk to them about something you take pretty seriously. How would you respond when that person asks for you to take their problems seriously? Not only would most people blow them off, they would be pretty pissed they even asked. Be aware that what you do in class will leave an impression with your professor. You need to respect what your professor feels is important if you ever hope for them to respect what you feel is important.

Office Hours

A professor's office hours is time that is set aside every week for helping students. Though mainly used for solving problems or explaining misunderstood concepts, this is also a time that can be used for professional networking or getting advice.

A professor's office hours may be the most underutilized resource on campus. I was as guilty as anyone of not taking advantage of this resource when I was starting out in college. Now that I am a professor I strongly encourage you not to follow in my footsteps. If you do not understand any aspect of the course you are taking and the person who has all the answers has set aside time to answer any and all questions, who's fault is it when your questions go unanswered? It's your fault. Sorry to be so blunt, but it's the truth. In the last two years of teaching in college I would estimate that of all the office hours I've held, maybe 5% of the time I've had a student in my office (and after polling dozens of professors, the 5% number holds pretty true). If all of my students were getting A's then I would have no problem, but a large portion of students earn C's, D's, or F's and no one asks questions. This is very puzzling. From my experience as a student I would have to say that the intimidation factor is probably the biggest hurdle to get over. Professors are people, just like you, your friends, and your parents. They go home at night and spend time with their families. My advice on this one is simple, make an appointment to see one of your professors and face your fear head on. Handle yourself professionally and you will see that professors are not people you should fear, but people you can use to help you achieve your career goal.

One other reason office hours are typically underutilized is the idea that professors are too busy to answer a simple question, so you just shouldn't ask them. This is a big misconception and an assumption you shouldn't make. Professors are professionals, if they're too busy, they will tell you they're too busy. Don't make this assumption; instead get good information directly from the source, the professor. Act professionally and you will get treated professionally. Most professors will go out of their way to accommodate you and find a time that can work with your schedule, even if it isn't during their normally scheduled office hours.

Communication with a Professor

The world has changed dramatically since the wide-scale use of technology such as the Internet, email, text messaging, and Facebook. When it comes to communicating with professors this technology can be both a blessing and a curse. I'm going to assume that most of the advice you've gotten about how to communicate with professors has not come from a professor. I would like to give you my advice on the subject from a professor's perspective.

The most common form of communication you're going to have with your professors, outside of the classroom, is email. Email has taken over as the main source of communication on most college campuses, and although it has some huge benefits, there can also be some big drawbacks that you should be aware of. I am going to assume you know the benefits, such as faster responses and writing replies at your convenience, so I want to address and advise you against some of the problems.

Advice on Email Communication with Your Professors

- NEVER forget that all emails with professors must be professional. Remember that professors belong in a different relationship category. You should <u>not</u> email professors the same way you email your friends or your family.

- Write a clear and direct subject in every email. Do not leave the subject blank. I know this may seem trivial, but there are a lot of "old school" professors that have had to learn email and are not the biggest fans of it.

- Properly address the professor. For example, if you were a student in one of my classes I would expect you to address me both in person and by email as Dr. Otter. Don't ever address a professor in an email as "Hey". I can tell you without a doubt this is not only completely unprofessional, it is down right insulting. Don't make this mistake and leave a bad impression with your professor.

- Sign your email. Be sure to put your name at the bottom of each email. Again, this sounds really simple, but students forget all the time. I know this isn't a big deal if you're emailing with friends or family, but this is different, this is professional, and it is a big deal.

- Use spell checker. All email systems have a version of spell checker, be sure to use it on every email. In the professional world there is no excuse for misspellings.

- Write, and then reread what you wrote before sending. A major luxury email gives you is the ability to take your time and write exactly what you want to say. Just like misspellings, there is no excuse for sentences that don't make sense.

- **NEVER** use text message language in an email. This is a major issue for a lot of professors and should never be used.

- Use a professional email address. I suggest always using the email address given to you by your college, but it is understandable if you prefer other types such as G-mail or Yahoo accounts. These accounts can offer services that most college email accounts can't, like unlimited space and unlimited attachment sizes. If you do choose to use an email address other than your college address, be very careful in the name you pick, it will leave an impression whether you want it to or not. Pick a professional sounding address for all emails with professors and any other professional contacts. Here is an example of an email sent to me my second year as a professor. I had a student ask if we could set a time to meet to discuss the material that would be on the final exam. The email had at least 10 misspellings, no punctuation, and the email was sent from <u>Hot-body_Tennessee69@yahoo.com</u> (name slightly changed to protect this persons identity – and so the guys reading this book don't try to look her up) and the email didn't contain the student's real name. Put yourself in my shoes, a professor's shoes....what would you think? What kind of impression does that leave?

Here is a good example of how an email communication with a professor should look. Always remember, the name of the game is professionalism.

From: smith4tt@mtsu.edu
To: <u>Otter@mtsu.edu</u>
Subject: Question about homework #4

Dr. Otter
My name is Amanda Smith. I am a student in Biology 101 class, section 4 and would like to schedule a time to discuss questions I have about homework #4. Unfortunately, I am in another class during your scheduled office hours. I am available to meet on Tuesdays after 3:00, Thursdays before 10:00 or after 5:00, and Fridays all day.
Thanks
Amanda Smith

Here is a bad example of the same email from Amanda's brother Marcus. This is not just an example, this is straight from my inbox last year.

From: smith7yc@mtsu.edu
To: Otter@mtsu.edu
Subject:

HEY! Homework 4 is tough Im not sure I now what to do.
Wheres ur office?

See the difference? One is written in a language that friends use to communicate, and the other is written in a language that professionals use to communicate. Both languages are perfectly acceptable ways to write email, but only one is an acceptable way to write an email to a professor.

What to Expect (and Not Expect) from Your Professors

Expectations of professors will vary depending on the type of class, the level of course, and the size of class you are in. Listed below are expectations you can have of all professors, regardless of the class you are taking. If any or all of your experiences exceed these expectations, do the professor a favor and let them know it.

- Expect your professor to start every class on time and not stop instructing until the class is scheduled to finish. Never plan on your professor dismissing class early.

- Expect your professors to treat you in a professional manner. Do not expect them to talk to you like a friend, family member or stranger. Any personal relationship you have with a professor should be considered special.

- Expect your professors to be in their office during their office hours. Do not expect them to be in their office any other time aside from that. Even though they likely will be, this is not an expectation you should have.

-Expect your professors to respond to email communication in a timely fashion (probably within 24-36 hours). Do not expect an immediate response. This means if you need an answer to something right away, you might not get it. So plan ahead and don't procrastinate.

- Expect your professors to clearly define what's expected of you (homework, exams, papers...etc) and how they're going to grade you. Whether you agree with their expectations and grading policy doesn't matter. *I'm sorry to put it so bluntly, but it's the truth.* This should all be clearly laid out in the syllabus (refer to the chapter on Classes for more information on what to expect on a syllabus).

It is reasonable to expect each of these things from every professor you encounter during college. If these expectations are not met, I would advise you to contact the professor directly to address the issue. Do so in a professional manner, and I'll be willing to bet your issue will be resolved. If, for some reason, after doing this you still have an issue, you should address your issue professionally with the chair of the department in which your professor works. Let me be very clear about this one. You should always try to resolve the issue directly with the professor in a professional manner first before taking any other course of action.

What Professors Expect from You

Similar to the expectations you should have of professors, professors have general expectations of students in their classes. Again, this will vary depending on the type of class, the level of course, and size of class you are in. Listed below are expectations professors have of you, regardless of the class you are taking.

- Professors expect students to be on time and to be engaged in the class. I know this can be a tough one especially in large and/or long classes, but like it or not, this is an expectation.

- Professors expect to be treated in a professional manner. This applies both in the classroom and outside of the classroom.

- Professors expect you to be on time to every meeting scheduled outside of class. If you have an appointment with a professor during or after office hours, it is fully expected that you will be on time and not be even one minute late. Punctuality is the very first impression you make with someone who doesn't know you. Be sure to be on the good side of that impression.

- Professors expect you to be responsible for yourself. Do not expect a professor to remind you that homework is due or that a test is coming up. If they do remind you, that's great, but once the class has been informed, it's your responsibility after that. If you miss class, it's your responsibility to find out what you missed. Professors will not re-lecture the material to you because you missed class and you shouldn't expect them to.

-Professors expect you to write in clear, correct English. I am a biology professor and I will mark down if someone is not writing in complete sentences or using proper grammar. At the college level, proper English is not just for English class. In addition, if you write with very small handwriting or very sloppy handwriting, work hard to write as clearly as possible. You should not expect a professor to try to decipher what you write.

As the old saying goes, "people fear what they don't understand." Hopefully now that I have explained how professors think you can understand why they do what they do. With this understanding I hope you won't be intimidated by professors, but use them for the valuable resources that they are.

Chapter 12
Friends

College is a time when you meet new people, try things you've never experienced before, and are independent probably for the first time. The people you choose to be around will help define your college experience. Ask anyone you know in college and aside from what major they've declared I'll guess they will talk about the people they've met, either at parties or in classes or in the Greek system. I personally met most of my best friends at college and stay in touch with them to this day. This is not that surprising when you really think about it. You will have more free time than you'll know what to do with and who you choose to spend that free time with and share your experiences with is something to think about. In this section, I want to give you advice on just a couple of things I've learned about the people you meet at college and the game of meeting friends.

- MEET NEW PEOPLE. No matter how many of your close friends go to the same college as you, make it a point to meet new people. As uncomfortable as it is to put yourself out there, it's worth it. Remember that other people are going through the same thing you are, especially if you are a freshman.

- BE YOURSELF. Surround yourself with people who are going to help you, both personally and professionally, but **above all else, be true to yourself**. I guarantee you will see and meet people that will do things you disagree with, people who inspire you, and people who are just plain strange. Use your gut feel and be true to yourself.

- BE OPEN-MINDED. This one fits hand-in-hand with being yourself. Once you understand yourself you will be more willing to talk, ask questions, and engage with people you disagree with or people you find strange. This, in my opinion, is what makes college so valuable. Personally, some of the best people I've ever met in my life are not like me at all and only when I was confident with myself was I willing to learn from other people. If you spend your whole life only talking to people just like you how much can you really learn? Not much.

- BE SELFISH. Be selfish about who you choose to spend your time with. You must be aware that you might end up changing the core group of friends you choose to be around. You are playing a new game with new rules, and with this new game may come new people. You should be selfish and purposely put yourself around people who can help you the most. If you have people around you who you *know* are hurting you and you <u>choose</u> to remain friends and give your time and energy to these people, that's your

<u>choice</u>. One of the many luxuries of college is that it brings people together from all over the place, not just your hometown.

Chapter 13
Classmates

Classmates are a great resource to help you in your classes. I can personally say that if it weren't for my fellow classmates in college I never would have succeeded professionally (or even passed a couple of classes). Students in the same class typically share a common goal, a good grade, which makes them more willing to help out other classmates. In the courses I teach I strongly encourage students to study in groups out of class, especially for exams, and I have seen a direct correlation between those who work in good study groups and good grades.

The main differences that separate a good study group from a bad study group are communication and professionalism. In order for a group of students to work well together each person in the group must be very clear about what they want to get out of the group. Next, each person in the group must be willing to help the other members of the group obtain their goals....even if everyone's goals aren't the same. Last, each person must approach the study group as a professional activity, not a meeting of friends. This point is typically the downfall of most study groups, especially if you are good friends with the other students in the group. If you work better in a study group, I suggest you find like-minded people in each of your classes and be a leader in forming a good study group. Every group needs a leader, so take charge, be organized, and everyone in the group will benefit.

Chapter 14
Counselors / Advisors

All colleges want you to succeed and graduate, and all colleges have academic advisors or counselors in place to help you with all your academic concerns. There is no difference between an advisor and a counselor; it really just depends on the terminology used at your college, so for this section I'm just going to refer to them as advisors. Some academic advisors may be your professors as well, while some may be 100% dedicated to the advising of students. In this section, I'm going to highlight what you should and shouldn't expect from an academic advisor.

You should expect an academic advisor to be a good source of information on which courses to take to fulfill your major, what necessary paperwork you need to fill out to be in good standing with the college, and to give you advice on the major you have chosen. Anything above and beyond these three things should be considered special and you should give them extra thanks for it. Please note, how I started the last sentence, they should be good sources of information; **advisors should not be making any decisions about your future**. That is 100% your responsibility and not something you should expect from an academic advisor. With that said, let's address the other things you shouldn't expect from an academic advisor. You should not expect an academic advisor to pick the classes you should be taking. You should not expect them to decide what major you should declare. You should not expect them to fill out any paperwork on your behalf.

All too often I hear the excuse that "my advisor just told to me to take this class and that's the only reason I am taking it." Advisors are exactly what their name means, someone that gives advice. In the end, you are 100% responsible for your decisions.

Academic advisors are wonderful resources of information. **I suggest you set an appointment with your advisor no less than one time each semester** to make sure you are on the right track and all the necessary paperwork is in order.

Chapter 15
Parents

You don't get to choose who your parents are, but with a mature mindset you do get to influence the type of relationship you have with them. Throughout this book I've been as honest as I can, and this section will be no different. In this section, I want to give you my honest advice about parents. It should come as no surprise that I believe the relationship you have with your parents has everything to do with your mindset.

Dealing with your parents is always a complicated situation. Let's face it they're your parents. You choose exactly how much you let them know and exactly how much you don't. Further, you can choose how much your parents influence your decisions. You should view yourself as a grown man or woman 100% responsible for everything you do. You choose what's best for you. With a kid's mindset, the choices are made for you and your future is in the hands of your parents. I advise you to deal with your parents with a mature mindset, make the decisions you think are right, and take complete responsibility for every decision you make. This means that if you get into trouble, you are 100% responsible for your mistakes, and if you do well, you get all the credit.

Your parents have known you longer than anyone else, and deep down, you know they want nothing but the best for you. Although they may want the best for you, this may not qualify them to give professional and unbiased advice on your future. Unless you are planning to follow in the exact foot-steps of your parents, you must recognize that they may not be a good source of professional advice.

In general, my advice for dealing with parents is simple, act the way you want to be treated. If you act like a kid around your parents, they will treat you like a kid. Handle yourself like a person with a mature mindset and *hopefully* your parents will treat you that way. I say hopefully, because ultimately your parents are people too, and you can't control anyone but yourself. **Focus on how *you* want to be more than how your parents want you to be.** Make decisions for yourself using good information and be proud of the decisions you make. You will be a kid in your parents' eyes forever, but that doesn't mean you have to act like one.

Section 4
Playing the Game

Chapter 16
This is Your Game

In this book, we have broken down the question of how to succeed at college into three major parts. We've dissected each of these parts so you know the tools and rules of the game, the other major players in the game, and a winning strategy for lifelong career success. In the end, however, the most important thing is how you put into practice what you've learned.

In the game of basketball, you can have the best strategy, know all the rules, and understand all the relationships with the other major players in the game and still lose, because in the end, it all comes down to execution. The game of college is exactly the same way, in the end, it all comes down to execution. When you compare how you play the game of basketball to how you play the game of college one major difference stands out. In basketball, you can only play one position at a time, but in the game of college you <u>must</u> play multiple positions at the same time. In other words, you need to be the player, coach, referee, a fan and a cheerleader all at the same time. As a coach, you need to devise a winning strategy. As a referee, you need to stay focused and force yourself to be honest. As a fan, you need to enjoy the process you are going through, and as a cheerleader, you need to stay positive and motivated. Last and most important, as a player, you need to execute your winning strategy. To play the game of college the best way possible you need to find the right balance between each of these positions. You also need to understand that each of these positions is your responsibility and that you can't wait for someone to fill these positions for you. This is a very tall order for any one person, but if you're trying to be great, it's going to take a great amount of work.

Unfortunately, there is no magic switch you can flip and be great at the game of college overnight. Just like any new game you're playing for the first time, it's going to take time for you to get comfortable and play the game well. Hopefully the information and advice I've given will help you decide how you want to play the game. **Whether you use the strategy discussed in this book or not, I hope you have a strategy to win at college.**

My goal in this book was to provide a good, universal real-world approach to college that can help all students, regardless of career path. After going over each of the major parts of the college game in detail, it's now up to you to put them together in the best way possible. There are no exercises to do to put all the parts together because your overall strategy on how you play the game of college is going to be unique to you. Set your goals high, rely on good information, take personal responsibility and choose to have a mature mindset. **This is your game and you need to be aggressive in the way you play**

it. Remember, you are a young professional with a mature mindset aggressively pursuing your career goal.

In this book, we have defined success at college as having a career goal and a strategic plan to achieve that goal by the time you graduate. If you focus on putting together the major parts covered in this book, you can not only succeed in the game of college, but you can set yourself up to enjoy working for the rest of your life in the career of your choice.

Two roads diverged in a wood, and I—
I took the one less traveled by,
And that has made all the difference.

- Robert Frost

CPSIA information can be obtained at www.ICGtesting.com
Printed in the USA
LVOW021401161112

307669LV00005B/5/P